Peter Behrens

Geboren den 14. April 1868
In Hamburg.
Im übrigen Autodidakt

Peter Behrens

Peter Behrens

Architect and Designer

Alan Windsor

WHITNEY LIBRARY OF DESIGN
an imprint of Watson-Guptill Publications, New York

First published in 1981 by
The Architectural Press Ltd.,
9, Queen Anne's Gate,
London SW1H 9BY

First published in the United States
and Canada by Whitney Library of
Design, an imprint of Watson-Guptill
Publications, a division of Billboard
Publications, Inc., 1515 Broadway,
New York, N.Y. 10036

**Library of Congress Cataloging in
Publication Data**
Windsor, Alan

Peter Behrens, Architect and Designer
Bibliography: P.
Includes Index.
1. Behrens, Peter, 1868–1940.
2. Artists—Germany—Biography.
3. Behrens, Peter,
1868–1940—Influence. I. Title
N6888.B433W56   1981   709'.2'4
(B)   81–12976
ISBN: 0 8230 7421 8   AACR2

Printed in Great Britain

Contents

FOR ELFRIEDE

Introduction

There is no doubt that Peter Behrens had a strong influence on the subsequent careers of his most famous assistants Walter Gropius, Ludwig Mies van der Rohe and Le Corbusier, and, through them and his other associates and pupils, on the whole course of architecture in the twentieth century. To some extent Behrens' career was a parallel in the field of architecture and design to that of Picasso in the world of painting and sculpture. Both experienced their first real success in the period of Art Nouveau and developed as artistic personalities within the ambience of the little art magazines that proliferated in Europe in the wake of the 'Studio', thus reaching a mass audience early. They both exhibited at the *Exposition Universelle* of 1900 in Paris, and both visited Paris for the first time to see their own work displayed in the sections representing the art of their respective countries. For both, 1907 was a turning-point in their artistic development, and both were subsequently the cynosure of all eyes. Both had the ability to absorb modes of expression pioneered by their contemporaries, and to use them instantly, often more brilliantly, so that they attracted and held more attention from the public than their less adroit fellows. Both were well publicized from early on in their careers; exhibitions, articles and books made their work widely known. Both were inexhaustibly prolific and eclectic, moving from one borrowed or invented style to another with bewildering speed. Sometimes they used several styles simultaneously.

Both turned, as did so many European artists, to classicism in the period just before and after the First World War, and yet both were susceptible to novel approaches—Expressionism in the case of Behrens, Surrealism in that of Picasso. Both, indeed, ran along a knife-edge of innovation and tradition, of setting the pace for their contemporaries, and yet in reality often doing little more than quickly and cleverly popularizing the ideas of others. Both were capable of remarkable achievement in many media, showing a rapid grasp of the potential of a new material or new subject. Meier-Graefe wrote of Behrens that 'no matter how assertively he might hold a particular position, he does not promise to hold it next time you meet; he will only promise to be better'. Whilst indifferent to the idea of 'doing better', Picasso for his part said, 'If the subjects I have wanted to express have suggested

1

different ways of expression, I have never hesitated to adopt them . . . different motives inevitably require different methods of expression.'

There perhaps the resemblance ends. Unlike the mercurial, anarchistic, bohemian painter, Peter Behrens was a methodical man, a conformist, a social conservative, a professorial figure with a life-long engagement in academic life, in administration and consultation. If the last ten years of his life were rendered more or less sterile by the violent distortion of social life in Germany at that period, his previous years appear to have been consistently devoted to a concept of life and art that was relatively benign and creative. Behrens was close to the centre of many of the most important developments in German culture between the 1890s and his death in 1940: his work and his writings are typical reflections of the artistic and spiritual aspirations of his time. Many historians have sought and found, in that period, nothing but evidence of the cultural bricks that ultimately built the Third Reich. For my part I have tried to sketch in the artistic, social, political and economic circumstances within which his work was done, as fairly but as briefly as possible. A reminder of such conditions is essential to an understanding of what the buildings or designs were actually about.

Behrens was a leading participant in the Art Nouveau and Arts and Crafts movements, after an initial training and career as a painter. He contributed to the development of the modern theatre; he was very active in graphic design, lettering and typography; he created a number of gardens; he was a self-taught architect, and designed a vast range of buildings, from embassies to workers' houses: he was the first major 'industrial designer'. As a teacher, he made an important contribution to the development of art education in Germany.

The aim of this book is to review the whole career of Peter Behrens, something that has not been done before in English. I have drawn heavily on Fritz Hoeber's monograph (1913), the excellent (unpublished) thesis for Columbia University by Stanford Anderson (1968); the exhibition catalogues for *Ein Dokument Deutscher Kunst* (1976); the more recent, exhaustive studies by Tilmann Buddensieg and Henning Rogge such as their *Industriekultur* (1979), and Hoepfner and Neumeyer's equally splendid *Das Haus Wiegand* (1979). Also important for me were Herta Hesse-Frielinghaus's *Karl Ernst Osthaus* (1977), Barbara Miller Lane's *Architecture and Politics in Germany, 1918–1945* (1968), and Joan Campbell's *The German Werkbund* (1978). I hope that the footnotes, references and the bibliography will point the interested reader in the direction of some of the books on Germany that I have found vital, even if they have only contributed a detail about Peter Behrens—Fritz Stern's *The Politics of Cultural Despair* (1961), for example, Harry Graf Kessler's elegiac *Tagebücher* or Karl Scheffler's *Die fetten und die mageren Jahre* (1946).

I would like to thank the staff of the *Akademie der Künste*, Berlin; Til Behrens, Frankfurt; Theodor Böll and others of the *Kunstbibliothek*, Berlin; Sherban Cantacuzino; Robert Cecil; Margaret Crowther; Professor Leonard

Eaton, Ann Arbor; Peter Fitzgerald; Anna-Christa Funk of the *Karl Ernst Osthaus Archiv*, Hagen; H. Haslauer, *AEG* Frankfurt; Robin Kinross; Hans-Werner Kluenner, *Bauhaus Archiv*, Berlin; the Staff of *Kraftwerk-Union*, Berlin; James Mosley, St Bride Printing Library, London; William Muschenheim, Ann Arbor; Stefan Muthesius, East Anglia; Peter Obst, *AEG* Berlin; Brian Petrie; Alfred Rowe; Christian Scheffler, *Klingspor-Museum*, Offenbach; Eckhard Siepmann, *Werkbund Archiv*, Berlin; Hedwig Singer, *Bundesarchiv*, Koblenz; M. Simon, *Firmenarchiv*, Hoechst; Daniel P. Simon, Berlin Document Center, Berlin; Albert Speer, Heidelberg; John Taylor; Jenny Towndrow; the Staff of the Wiener Library, London; Susan Wheeler; Eva Wirtz, *AEG Firmenarchiv*, Braunschweig; Margaret Porter and William Moritz, California; the Research Board of the University of Reading, and the *Deutscher Akademischer Austauschdienst* who kindly gave me grants for travel in Germany; to Kerry and Margaret Downes, who were generous in reading, advising and correcting; and, finally, my wife who gave me constant encouragement, criticism and help.

1 Early Life and Career

Peter Behrens was born on 14 April 1868 in St Georg, Hamburg. His father, a well-to-do landowner from Langenhals in Holstein, who was already in his sixties, did not marry the young Louise Margaretha Burmeister, mother of his heir, and died before the child was six. At the age of fourteen, Peter Behrens was taken into the care of a guardian, Senator Sieveking, as his mother had also died.[1] The Sievekings were and still are one of the most prominent families of Hamburg. Behrens inherited a great deal of money from his father, and so was familiar from childhood with privilege, influence and wealth; that, and the early deaths of his parents, gave him an awareness of the need to control his own destiny. Citizens of Hamburg pride themselves on their reserve and self-reliance: Behrens always retained what Gropius described years later as 'the cool demeanour of a conservative Hamburg patrician'; Karl Scheffler recalled him as 'always having a somewhat Senatorial air'.[2]

On leaving school in Altona he chose to study art, and attended the *Gewerbeschule*, Hamburg, the *Kunstschule*, Karlsruhe (1886) and then studied as a private pupil with the Hamburg artist Ferdinand Brütt in Düsseldorf. A little later (1889) he moved to Munich and studied under Hugo Kotschenreiter. At twenty-one he married Elisabeth (Lilli) Krämer, a girl from Ochsenfurt, one year younger than himself. They settled in 69 Georgenstrasse. The photograph of them at this time shows Behrens, well dressed, towering a full head taller than his pretty wife.

Munich was then the major centre of artistic activity in Germany. At first, Behrens' painting followed the example of the older generation of Realists and Impressionists (Wilhelm Leibl, for example, or Max Liebermann) who had been responsible for introducing French and Dutch influences into German painting in recent years. Behrens visited Holland in 1890, and met Jozef Israels, a leading figures of the *Luministen*, the Dutch group of painters who were concerned with effects of light and who were much admired in Munich circles. He also worked alongside Albert Neuhuis.

A painting of 1891, *'Entlassen'* ('Dismissed'), shows a workman against the gloomy background of a railway siding at nightfall; a factory is also in the background. *'In Gedanken'* ('In Thought'), of the same year, is of a seated

Peter and Lilli Behrens. Photograph, c 1889.

man at the window of a darkened room. *'Feierabend'* of 1892 is a harbour scene, again dark, with dim lights sparkling on the water below the steel structures and factory chimneys of a quayside. It is curious that these earliest paintings of Behrens are *Armeleutemalerei*—paintings of poor people—and scenes of industrial landscape; they anticipate his engagement with the real industrial world later in life.

Fellow northerners in Munich with whom Behrens became particularly friendly were Otto Eckmann, also from Hamburg, and Hans Olde, a Holsteiner. Both these artists painted in subdued, closely harmonious tones, creating luminous effects of colour and light. Behrens' style developed under their influence, and entered a lighter phase where subject matter is concerned. He took part in the Munich *Sezession* of 1892: the first formal, organized secession of artists from a German Academy. (It was led by Franz von Stuck, and included Uhde, Corinth, Trübner, Segantini, Israels and others.) In the first *Sezession* exhibition, 1893, Behrens showed *'Zecher bei gelbem Lampenlicht'* ('Toper by yellow lamplight'); in this picture, the yellow gaslight competes with the blue of dawn seen through the window. It was

5

exhibited at the *Grosse Berliner Kunstausstellung* later the same year, and attracted an enormous amount of attention, as it was popularly seen as a foil to Max Klinger's *'Die blaue Stunde'* ('The Blue Hour'). According to Karl Scheffler (the art critic) the two pictures became a great talking point—Klinger's picture being known as 'Blue Happiness' and Behrens' wretched drinker as 'Blue Gloom'.

But by this time Behrens had, on the whole, moved away from Social Realism. Two other pictures shown in the 1893 *Sezession* were *'Vorfrühling'* ('Early Spring'), a composition of three young girls dressed in violet, red and green, dancing in a clearing in a wood, and *'Abend'* ('Evening'), a young girl in green by a violet flowering tree. These are much more Eckmann-like subjects.

During 1894 and 1895, however, Behrens painted a large number of small landscapes, executed out-of-doors in an Impressionist manner. In 1896 he visited Italy for the first time.

The playwright Otto Erich Hartleben wrote on 3 April to his wife Selma from Florence: '. . . I had a Mr Behrens, a painter from Munich, as travelling companion; he is going on further alone . . .'[3] They had left Munich together on 21 March, and their first experience of Italy together sealed a warm friendship that lasted until Hartleben's early death in 1905. Glimpses of their shared high spirits can be seen in Hartleben's effervescent and charming letters, both immediately after their joint introduction to Italy and over the years to come; they are full of fun and references to drinking sessions. A postcard from Chiusi to Behrens, presumably sent just after they had parted company, wittily parodied Nietzsche's *'Das Trunkene Lied'* ('The Drunken Song') from *Also Sprach Zarathustra*:

I wake from deepest sleep: With wine
to wreck the night had been my crime
I laughed until past midnight—
A new mid-day now is high.
Light already? O Yes, think I:—
The Rising Sun's already bright
A quick vermouth and so
I get my shaky limbs to go.[4]

Hartleben's works at that time were lighthearted and skilful erotic comedies, many with a classical or Neo-Hellenic basis. His subsequent success enabled him to live much of the time in Italy for the rest of his life. For Behrens, the trip laid the foundation of a life-long devotion to Italy; from then on he spent long holidays there more or less every year. His friendship with lively and amusing characters like Hartleben and Otto Julius Bierbaum and other writers associated with the magazine *Pan* must have made this one of the happiest periods of his life. He painted Hartleben's portrait (1898) and, in 1903, made of it one of his biggest woodcuts. In the summer of 1900, Behrens designed a dining-room for Hartleben, who wrote:

Portrait of O. E. Hartleben. Woodcut,
53·5 × 39·5 cm (21 × 15½ in), 1903.

Portrait of Richard Dehmel. Woodcut,
46 × 30·7 cm (18 × 12 in), 1903.

Portrait of Bismarck. Woodcut,
35·2 × 24·6 cm (13¾ × 9½ in), 1899.

'Winterlandschaft'. Woodcut,
26·6 × 21·2 cm (10¼ × 8¼ in), 1899.

Your dining-room is now finished and delights all eyes. Over the side-table swoops the Eagle [one of Behrens' woodcuts—'*Sturm*', which he had given to Hartleben the previous year] and your portrait of me hangs over the sideboard.[5]

Behrens designed another dining-room a little later (1903) for a mutual friend, the poet Richard Dehmel. This also was decorated with large woodcuts—'The Kiss' and 'Butterflies on waterlilies'.[6]

On his return from Italy, Behrens turned to studio compositions of a more Symbolist kind in reaction against Impressionism and Realism. He took up the woodcut as a medium, and treated it in the newly fashionable manner derived from Japanese prints. The woodcut had of course been

Natalie Clifford Barney and Eva Palmer. Photograph, 1894(?).

revived in recent years in France by Gauguin, Felix Vallotton and others, while the flat, linear and evenly coloured style of print popularised by

'Sturm'. Woodcut, 49·5 × 65 cm (19 × 25½ in), 1896.

'Der Kuss'. Woodcut, 27·2 × 21·7 cm (10½ × 8½ in), 1898. The work was possibly inspired by the photograph opposite (top).

French colour-lithographers was being exploited in Germany by such graphic artists as Walter Leistikow. Many of Behrens' woodcuts were exceptionally large. Typical examples are *'Sturm'* of 1896 (49·5 × 65 cm), *'Schmetterlinge auf Seerose'* (50 × 64 cm) of the same year, and *'Der Kuss'* (27·2 ×21·7 cm) of 1898.

This last, a six-colour woodcut, has long been recognized as typical of the genre—a favourite motif for reproduction in books and articles on Art Nouveau. It first appeared in reproduction in Julius Meier-Graefe's magazine *Pan* for which Behrens had begun to submit regular contributions of graphic work.

Perhaps inspired by Rodin's famous sculpture (then about ten years old, and on exhibition in the *Salon de la Société Nationale* about the time of Behrens' woodcut), it is a rather daring subject for the period: a kiss on the mouth is

'Ein Traum'. Tempera or Silikat pastel, 1897.

very rare in art before 1898. The woodcut by Munch was an obvious recent precedent, but was treated very differently. Perhaps Behrens derived his image from a photograph of Natalie Clifford Barney kissing her friend Evalina Palmer (1894?). The shapes of the eyes, noses, mouths, chins and throats are more or less identical; the left hand figure is dark, the right hand one fair, and so on. Perhaps the perennial fascination of the woodcut lies in its ambiguity: drained of all passion, and reduced to the threshold of becoming pure pattern, the two profiles of indeterminate sex are disturbing in their pale, mirror-like similarity. Whether it was intended to be of lesbians or not, the woodcut remains an isolated excursion into the 'decadent' for Behrens; perhaps he did not even realize the implications of the image.

It was not the same Behrens who cut the '*Winterlandschaft*' (a view of the porch of St Andreas in Hildesheim) or the vigorous portrait of Bismarck (who had recently died) in 1899. The portraits of his friends Dehmel and Hartleben, executed a little later, again used the engraving tool to create strong and dramatic modelling in light and shade.

His three major paintings of 1897 were the so-called 'Iris Portrait', a three-quarter length portrait of his wife Lilli, her dress, the background and the stencilled frame of the picture being decorated with iris motifs; a decorative painting, '*Die Trauer*' ('Sorrow') of a seated woman with long hair, rather in the manner of Hodler; and a large canvas, '*Ein Traum*' ('A Dream') painted in a medium which gives a tempera or fresco-like appearance to the paint by fixing the colours with silica, a technique popular in Germany in the late nineteenth century.

It depicts a naked youth, a violin in his right hand, lying asleep on the ground. From his side rises a thinly veiled girl looking heavenwards with a radiant face. In this painting, vaguely evocative of Botticelli's 'Venus' or Michelangelo's 'Creation of Eve', some of Behrens' life-long characteristics of design are already found: he favoured closed, static forms, centralized and symmetrically placed, with an underlying geometrical basis for their composition.

The Arts and Crafts Movement

About this time Behrens began to extend the range of his artistic activity to include the design of porcelain, glass and furniture. His activity as a painter gradually declined. He was drawn into the group that formed the *Vereinigten Werkstätten für Kunst im Handwerk* (United Studios for Art in Handicraft), and participated in their first exhibition at the *Glaspalast* in Munich in 1899. (Other leading figures were August Endell, Hermann Obrist, Martin Dülfer, Richard Riemerschmid, Bernhard Pankok and Bruno Paul). Behrens' friend Otto Eckmann had led the way by giving up painting, and having a spectacular sale of his pictures in 1894 to mark the end of his career as a 'fine artist'.

In 1898, Behrens designed an elegant range of wineglasses—a set of twelve types—made by Benedikt von Poschinger at Oberzwieslau, and an

Tea Service, red decoration on white, 1901.

attractive range of white plates decorated with various patterns, carried out by Villeroy and Boch of Mettlach. In 1899, he designed some pieces of 'art' pottery and glass, an outstanding example being the glass vase manufactured by Rindkopfs Söhne of Nordböhmen. A series of vases was made in 1900 by Mehlem of Bonn. In 1901 these individual pieces were followed up with the design of full tea, coffee and dinner services, usually in white porcelain with green, blue and red decoration.

In silverware, Behrens designed jewellery carried out by Schreger of Darmstadt, and services of cutlery executed by M. J. Rückert of Mainz. This firm later carried out the thirteen-piece service designed for the Behrens house in Darmstadt, as well as a design with crossed-over tendrils, for the exhibition *Ein Dokument Deutscher Kunst* in 1901.

His furniture designs seem to have begun with a range of cherry-wood chairs, stools and settles in 1900, with the kitchen and dining-room for Hartleben mentioned earlier, and with such individual items as a decorated cot for the baby of Dr Walter Harlan, one of Hartleben's friends. A little later he made one or two excursions into *Reformkleidung*: rational dress, without corsets or stays, for women.[7]

It was this activity as a *Kunstgewerbeler*, an applied artist, that earned Behrens an exhibition in Darmstadt, and membership of the *Künstlerkolonie*.

Notes

1. Details of Behrens' family tree and that of his wife can be found in the *Ahnentafel* he submitted to the *Akademie der Künste* in Berlin, 14 August 1933.

2. Walter Gropius, *Apollo in der Demokratie*, Mainz und Berlin, Florian Kupferberg, 1967, pp124–5, and Karl Scheffler, *Die fetten und die mageren Jahre*, Leipzig, List, 1946, pp34–40.
3. Otto Erich Hartleben, *Briefe an seine Frau 1887–1905* Berlin, Fischer, 1908, p211.
4. Otto Erich Hartleben, *Briefe an Freunde*, Berlin, Fischer, 1912. The German is as follows:

Aus tiefem Schlaf bin ich erwacht . . .
Die Nacht hab ich beim Wein verbracht,
hab über Mitternacht gelacht-
-nun blüht ein Mittag wieder.
Ist es schon hell?—Ich denke, ja.—
Der Klaps aus Japan ist schon da.
Schnell einen Vermuth, denn der Ta-
-tterich belebt die Glieder (p230).

Behrens designed many title-pages for Hartleben's books in the 1890s. See Alfred von Klement, *Die Bücher von O. E. Hartleben*, 1951. When in Berlin, Hartleben presided over a *Stammtisch*, a regular social meeting of artists and writers, to which Behrens occasionally came. August Strindberg and Paul Scheerbart (author of *Glasarchitektur*) also attended.
5. Hartleben, *Briefe an Freunde*, p274.
6. Mentioned by Dehmel in a letter to Behrens. This and other references to things designed for him by Behrens, are in his *Ausgewählte Briefe 1883–1902*, Berlin, Fischer, 1922 and those of *1902–1920*, Berlin, Fischer, 1923.
7. See Heinrich Pudor, *Reform Kleidung*, Leipzig, 1903.

2 Behrens at Darmstadt

In 1900, Darmstadt was a growing city of about 72,000 inhabitants. An ancient market town, it was also the capital city of Hesse, and had been the seat of the Counts and Dukes of Hesse for several centuries. In the early nineteenth century, the town was greatly extended: the *Grossherzog* Ludewig I employed his court architect, Georg Moller, to create an elegant new quarter of neo-classical domestic and public buildings, on a strict grid-iron plan. The town was further enlarged as the century progressed, and, with the coming of the railways, industries grew up on the fringes of the city on a modest scale: a chemical industry, the manufacture of machinery and boilers; and lighter industries, such as furniture, ceramics, printing and bookbinding. The furniture manufacturers (Glückert, Alter, Trier) were well known nationally and internationally. The population was employed variously at Court, in the Government, the Civil Service, in trade, commerce and industry.

The Künstlerkolonie

Grossherzog Ernst Ludwig von Hessen und bei Rhein (1868–1937), the initiator of the Darmstadt *Künstlerkolonie*, was a constitutional ruler, and was served in government by an elected *Landtag*. He was the son of Alice, Queen Victoria's favourite daughter, and his grandmother frequently visited Darmstadt. Following the early death of his mother, Victoria supervised his education. Almost every year during his childhood he spent some time in his second, English, home. A liberal in his political outlook (nicknamed 'The Red Grand Duke') he was regarded generally as an English Gentleman and a German patriot in one: Harry Graf Kessler, who was a fellow student at Leipzig University wrote: 'Of all German Princes he was in the most natural way a European and a man of the world'. Alfred Lichtwark (the Hamburg Art Gallery Director) characterized him as having 'the urbanity of a German officer of rank and the artistic culture of a modern English Gentleman'.[1]

He succeeded to the Grand Duchy in 1892, at the age of twenty-three, and reigned until the 1918 Revolution. Perhaps stimulated by the example of his grandfather Albert in England, he determined to take an energetic part in the development of Darmstadt as a centre of new social and cultural activity.

He was encouraged to do so with enthusiasm by his subjects. On his accession, the Darmstadt writer Georg Fuchs, for example, published an anonymous article as a broadsheet:

Was erwarten die Hessen von ihrem Grossherzog Ernst Ludwig? —*von einem ehrlichen, aber nicht blinden Hessen.* ('What do the people of Hesse expect of their Grand Duke Ernst Ludwig?—by a loyal, but not blind, subject.)

In this, Fuchs exhorted him, with much emphasis, to patronize the arts.

One of Ernst Ludwig's first actions regarding art and architecture was to abandon the prizewinning designs for a Ducal Museum (prepared by Schmieden and Speer, 1892) and to give the job to Alfred Messel, who was to develop the Grand Duke's own ideas. In 1897–8 he employed the English architects Hugh Mackay Baillie-Scott and Charles Robert Ashbee to design interiors for his *Residenz*, the *Neue Palais*. Otto Eckmann, Behrens' friend from Munich, was also called in to design Ernst Ludwig's private study-cum-workroom in the palace in 1897. Fuchs had the satisfaction of seeing Ernst Ludwig as the first Prince of the ancient Ducal house to 'fuse life and art together'.

In September 1898 the first exhibition of the *Freien Vereinigung Darmstädter Künstler* (the Free Alliance of Darmstadt Artists) opened in the *Kunsthalle*, under the patronage of the Duke. The exhibition included applied art, and the *Kunstgewerbe* section was organized by the Darmstadt publisher Alexander Koch. Koch owned a wallpaper factory in Darmstadt, was another Anglophile and a tireless advocate of the importance of applied art. He had begun publishing as early as 1888, with the *Deutsche Tapetenzeitung*; in 1890 he followed this with the *Zeitschrift für Innendekoration*, and in May 1897 he produced *Deutsche Kunst und Dekoration*, closely modelled on the *Studio* magazine. Georg Fuchs was his secretary.

On the first page of the first issue of *Deutsche Kunst und Dekoration*, Koch had appealed to German artists and patrons for 'genuine, great artists [to work for] the lesser arts'. He drew attention to

The need for a complete integration of all artists, architects, sculptors, painters and craftsmen. They all belong intimately together in the same place, each thinking individually yet working together hand-in-hand for a larger whole.

He followed this up at the close of the 1898 exhibition in the *Kunsthalle* with a memorandum to the Grand Duke and to one or two Cabinet Ministers. In this memorandum, entitled *'Darmstadt: A City of Art?'*, Koch made out his case for Darmstadt as *the* German city which might become a leading centre of applied art; it included proposals for homes and ateliers for artists. Koch argued that

Other than in Munich, there is no centre for this kind of art, which is growing so strongly, and which, as the example of England, Belgium, Holland, France demonstrates, will in the near future play a major role in the life of the nation.

15

The seizure of the opportunity to encourage influential artists and young talent would establish an institution of lasting worth and of the greatest spiritual and material value, he said.

Behind the altruistic enthusiasm for the Arts and Crafts movement lay a real but discreetly understated hope that local light industry would benefit materially; moreover

The encouragement of artistic handicraft is extremely important, not only from an aesthetic point of view but also from that of political economy, as it brings substantially more money to the common people than does so-called 'High Art' (painting and sculpture) and creates contented folk.[2]

The memorandum was presented in November, to coincide with the opening of a museum of applied art (the *Gewerbemuseum*) in Neckarstrasse. The idea for an artists' colony gathered support from politicians and businessmen. In a debate of the Second Chamber of the *Landstände* it was said that '. . . from the development of the colony, practical models and useful material, repercussions on the productive capability of our domestic applied art industry . . .' might be obtained. The First Chamber of the *Landstände* eventually offered the sum of 20,000 marks in support of the scheme.[3] This financial support was to be annual, but limited to a period of three years:

. . . if it were not viable by then it could not be further supported . . . either the colony will stand on its own feet after this period or not; in either case further subsidy will have to depend on the outcome.

The moving spirit of the Darmstadt project was, therefore, a novelty. Earlier artists' colonies (such as Worpswede near Bremen) had been private, self-motivated, financily self-supporting, relatively informal and spontaneous affairs, but the Darmstadt venture was planned and launched not by artists themselves, but by Ducal, State and Industrial initiative. The artists were to enjoy the patronage of the Grand Duke and the city on a scale of munificence and security unparalleled even in the Renaissance.

Darmstadt, wrote Georg Fuchs, was to become the 'smiling third' art city of Germany, alongside Munich and Berlin.

The beginning of the Künstlerkolonie
At the beginning of December 1898, the painter Hans Christiansen, who had been strongly featured by Koch in his exhibitions, was the first artist to be invited to the proposed artists' colony. Christiansen was a prolific and versatile artist who designed furniture, stained glass, ceramics, glassware, tapestries and graphics as well as painting his canvasses. At the beginning of April 1899, the colony was made public as the subject of a series of articles in the *Darmstädter Tageblatt*; at the same time three other artists were formally invited to join the colony. They were Rudolf Bosselt, a sculptor and designer

16

of coins and medals; Paul Bürck, a painter who also did book decorations and other applied art, and Patriz Huber, an interior decorator and designer of furniture: all associates of Alexander Koch.

The exact nature of the individual contracts for the first artists to be called to Darmstadt is not known (the archives of the *Künstlerkolonie* were destroyed by bombing on 11–12 September 1944), but essentially the contract was for three years, with an annual grant or salary, the provision of land on very advantageous terms and a subsidy towards the cost of building. In theory the artists were to be allowed to work without special regard to manufacture or sale, following their individual paths. They were not required to do any teaching. In principle they had freedom to take on special commissions, or to have private pupils. Travel for educational, cultural or business reasons was permitted. The colony was to be characterized as a 'free creative community . . . with no differences of rank'.

Behrens as one of the 'Seven'

On 3 June 1899, an exhibition of the work of Peter Behrens opened at the *Kunsthalle* and in July he was invited to join the four artists already chosen. He, along with Ludwig Habich the sculptor (and only native of Darmstadt) and Joseph Maria Olbrich, the Viennese architect, made up the Darmstadt 'Seven', a group of young artists aged between twenty-one and thirty-three years.

In November, the artists presented the Grand Duke with an Address, designed and decorated by Behrens. This outlined their artistic programme, including, most importantly, the plan for an exhibition, *Ein Dokument deutscher Kunst* (A document of German art) to take place in 1901. It was, in effect, not so much an artistic manifesto—several of the artists published statements of their artistic credo in magazine articles over the ensuing months—as a statement of intent, most of which had no doubt been agreed in advance with the Grand Duke. The general intention was to present 'a lasting picture of modern culture and modern artistic feeling'. The building programme was outlined: there was to be a workshop; a hall for the exhibition of the most interesting creations of the colony; an exhibition hall for graphic art and one for theatrical interpretations. Above all, the building of model family houses would demonstrate in toto their artistic principles. They would design 'Family houses which in their simple, fully developed entireties will convincingly express the basic principles of our artistic feelings.' These houses were to be built on the *Mathildenhöhe*, a little hill belonging to the Grand Duke, to the north-east of the old town.[4]

The first undertaking of the *Künstlerkolonie* was an interior in the German pavilion of the Paris *Exposition Universelle* of 1900. Behrens contributed some of his woodcuts, some bookbindings and decorative detailing. This interior, largely executed by the Darmstadt firm of Julius Glückert, was a sensation partly for its modernity and partly because, unlike the majority of the exhibits at the Fair, it was not just a heterogeneous collection of objects without reference to each other, but a unified interior, the product of a novel artistic collaboration. In August, Behrens paid his first visit to Paris. Julius Meier-Graefe met him there, and recalled that Behrens was enthusiastic about the 'primitive' works of art there, from the Orient and from Egypt; he had, however, no interest at all in the collections of European painting.

Behrens' house on the Mathildenhöhe

Behrens was now thirty-two years old, and entering a period of tremendously varied activity, and one in which his approach would decisively change from being that of a competent, if unadventurous, painter, an Art Nouveau graphic artist with an interest in the crafts, to becoming a self-taught architect and industrial designer.

The deed for the sale of land to Peter Behrens was made out in July 1900 and entitles him 'Professor'; he was so styled for the rest of his life. His house, the only one of the colony not designed by Olbrich, was to be at once a dwelling and an exhibit in the forthcoming *Ausstellung* of 1901; a statement of a way of living and a model of style. The building land and the cost of building the houses had to be paid for by the artists themselves; the raising of capital for this was in part done by the artists in anticipation of their expected commissions and sales at the exhibition. The building cost of the villas was on average about 40,000 marks, and the interior decoration, furnishing and fittings came to about 30,000 marks. The least extravagant house—Olbrich's—cost a total of about 30,000 marks, while Behrens' was the most expensive, at 200,000 marks.[5]

The house was built on the Alexandra Weg, which runs roughly east-west along the slope of the *Mathildenhöhe*. The exterior is not unlike the traditional housing of the North German coast and of the frontiers with Holland and Denmark, having a rather Dutch-looking gable dominating the façade, and decorative pilaster strips, quoins and architraves that may be taken to paraphrase half-timbering. These are executed in emphatically moulded green-glazed bricks against pure white rendered wall surfaces. The roof is covered with vigorous red tiles. The chimneys are tall and slightly Tudor in style. Over the hall window on the garden side runs an inscription (possibly from Dehmel): *'Steh' Fest, Mein Haus, im Weltgebraus!'* ('Stand fast, my house, in the world's tumult!')

In form, the house is more or less a cube—early evidence of Behrens' predilection for solid geometry in architecture. Internally, there are three floors on the garden, or south, side, above a semi-basement containing the kitchen. Over the dining-room was the bedroom of Mrs Behrens, and in the attic, a guest bedroom and one for their son Josef. (The Behrens' had two children by then, both born in Munich: Josef, born 1890, and Petra, born 1898.) At the front of the house, facing north, the rooms are taller, making only two floors: the music room and, above that, Behrens' studio.

On the ground floor, the house has a simple and compact plan, with an entrance hall from which the staircase rises, with wide sliding screens

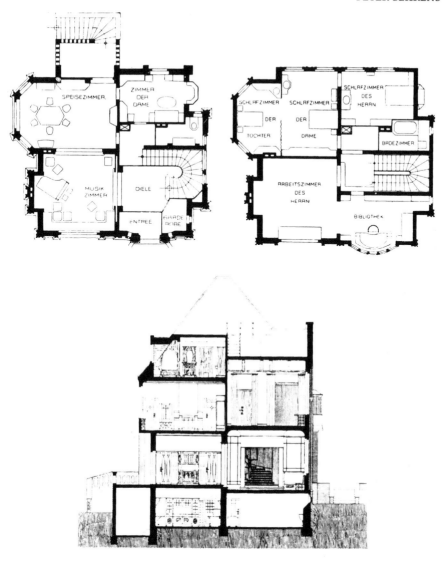

Behrens' House, Darmstadt, 1901: Ground plan (top left); First floor plan (top right); Section (above).

opening from it into the music room, which is in turn interconnected with the dining room through a wide arch. Beyond this was a ladies' drawing room.

In this way, almost the whole of the ground floor could be opened to make a continuous space for, for example, musical evenings. He planned it so that the inhabitants of his house had the maximum possibility for privacy, if they so wished, and yet could easily collect together when desired. The

19

ground plan has been compared with that of Frank Lloyd Wright's first house—also for himself and his family—at Oak Park, of the previous year. (Wright was a near contemporary of Behrens incidentally; he, Lutyens and Matisse were born the year after Behrens.)

As Morton Shand has written:

Behrens linked his rooms together in an organic, unstylistic unity, in a far more forthright and uncompromising manner than Van de Velde had yet dared to do . . . he revealed himself as a master of *'Raumgestaltung'* . . . the spatial design of rooms, as opposed to the solid surfaces circumscribing them.[6]

The music room was regarded as the heart of the ground floor of the house. Behrens wrote:

In order that the music room . . . really the principal apartment of the house—should be loftier than the rooms surrounding it, it was necessary to place the floor two steps below that of the entrance passage, and to raise the ceiling, by about as much, above the adjoining dining-room.[7]

The music room was dark and intense, with much intarsia-work in dark wood; there were armchairs, stools and benches of black-stained birch; a gilded ceiling 'like some old church dome'; blue mirror-glass on walls decorated with red and grey marble, and a grand piano of grey-stained maple stood in a niche below the large painting *'Ein Traum'* of 1897. This painting remained one of Behrens' favourite works, and was given a prominent place in his Neubabelsberg house, years later. On either side of the niche stood tall candelabra, and on either side of the opening to the dining-room the piers were decorated with stylized figures, like Egyptian goddesses, bearing crystals radiating light. (The lid of the piano had the Egyptian motif of spread wings.) The floor of this room was inlaid with a crystalline pattern of expensive woods.

The solemn, sacral atmosphere of this room was emphasized by Behrens in the little catalogue of his house, which was available to visitors during the exhibition. He explained, for example, that the 'spiritual need' of the steps between the music room and the dining-room was 'to lend a rhythmical movement to passage between the two rooms'. This sort of thing, not surprisingly, irritated some observers. 'How many mortals could sense the various interpretations placed by Behrens on the way one treads the steps between the dining-room and the music room?' asked the *Darmstädter Tageblatt*. In the magazine *Jugend*, a little poem appeared:

The stairs' integral mystery
A secret still to you would be
Had Behrens not the meaning shown;
Made clear, in mild instructive tone.[8]

In sharp contrast to the music room was the dining-room, with japanned white furniture and panelling and silver and crystal electric light fittings

Behrens' House: Dining room

over the white dining-table and chairs; the carpet and other accents were wine red.

A door opened on to a terrace from which steps descended to the garden. The ladies' drawing-room, to the side of the dining-room, was furnished and decorated with polished birchwood, and the decorative scheme was predominantly yellow.

Upstairs were two principal bedrooms, one for Mrs Behrens, in polished lemon-wood, and with yellow silk curtains and bedspread. This had a section that could be partitioned off to make a bedroom for a small child. (Petra Behrens was two years old). The other bedroom, for Behrens, was in violet-japanned poplar.

The painter's studio, which had the beams of the roof exposed on its ceiling, a library opening off it, and a bathroom completed the floor. The attic contained a guest room and a bedroom for the son. The attic rooms were wholly lined—ceiling, walls and floor—with natural pine. Behrens wrote of it:

With the layout of the guest room on the top floor, the principle of 'privacy where needed' was most markedly applied. Here, the guest may have, to a degree, all living comforts at his disposal, in miniature. As the roof supports were used for the

Behrens' House: Studio.

22

subdivision of the little apartment, it provides, with a living room and a bedroom, an independence of others in the household.

These attic rooms had gas fires, although the rest of the house was centrally heated from a boiler in the basement.

The interior of the house was a remarkable tour-de-force of integrated designs in many media, including wood, marble, glass, ceramics, metal and textiles. The carpets, wall panels, ceilings, doors, light fittings, furniture, cutlery, glass, china and linen were all designed by Behrens. Inevitably, one is reminded of the example set by Henry van de Velde, whose recently constructed house *Bloemenwerf* (1896–7) at Uccle, Brussels, had been widely publicized in Germany; notably in Meier-Graefe's second number of *Dekorative Kunst* (1898–99). Echoes of *Bloemenwerf* may indeed be considered to be recognizable in the gables and some of the window-shapes of Behrens' house. His dining-room chairs, at any rate, are remarkably like those of Van de Velde at Uccle.

In various articles at this time—in his little brochure about the house, in the *Hauptkatalog* of the exhibition and elsewhere—Behrens made considered statements of his intentions in the design of his house and in his participation in the colony. These ranged from the particular to the general.

In the house erected by myself, I was constrained by local conditions to confine the area of the ground plan to the utmost possible extent, and, on the other hand, compelled to provide the rooms required for the accommodation of an average family.

On that account the rooms had to be arranged in a way providing for convenient intercommunication between the rooms that belong together by reason of the purpose they serve. My idea was that members of the family should have the opportunity of being together or of retiring into privacy, just as they pleased. This was effected by a system of rooms of different dimensions . . .

In general terms he wrote:

Architecture is the art of building, and comprises in its name two ideas; the mastery of the practical, and the art of the beautiful. There is something exhilarating in being able to combine in one word the two ideas—that of practical utility and that of abstract beauty—which unfortunately have too often been opposed to each other. But we have left that time behind us, and we may affirm with satisfaction that the indications of conciliation are becoming more pronounced. The practical object does not seem to us to be any longer entirely subservient to mere utility, but combines therewith a certain degree of pleasure. Efforts were made formerly to relieve the bareness of everyday utility by embellishing it, adding ornaments to plain, serviceable objects, and hiding the mere prosaic purpose . . . Then came the realization of physical pleasure existing in the useful and the suitable, and by degrees people wanted to see the intention, to observe the suitability of things . . . This development of artistic perception, combined with the progress made in our technique and newly discovered materials, is at once a guarantee of the fertility of the modern style and its justification. Thus we shall now be able, owing to the combination of the two ideas of art, to speak of architecture corresponding in the highest degree with the spirit of the time . . .

In his opinion, the 'Seven' were persuaded that they were living at a time in which a new era was beginning. He believed, with them, that applied art was to be ranked with the other forms of art, and that there was no distinction between the arts. Most important in architecture and design were, he considered, the purpose (*Zweck*) and the construction. He advocated forms 'which invite use' ('*Die zum Gebrauch einladen*'). In Darmstadt, he wanted to see 'every conceivable area of art, technique and industry' considered. In approaching Nature as a mentor, he advised that

It isn't from individual forms in nature that we can deduce a useful pattern or model, but from its structure, its construction . . . the mighty law of nature.

At Darmstadt he saw the development of 'a new style, surpassing that known to us' as a real possibility. He wanted to see 'art enjoyed in the sense that all life needs the beautiful, and beauty gives everyone life'. The whole of life, indeed, should become 'a great, equally valued form of art. . . . Life itself should be once more a Style.'

The house was well received on the whole, and in the spirit in which it was intended that it should. Felix Commichau, for example, wrote

Behrens creates from the principle of making a thorough examination of the innermost essence of each task. . . . Through and through a 'modern man', Behrens, in what he has presented, has given a truly new work of art—each work as from the same mould. There are no false notes; all is one form from the base to the roof . . . Whether the decoration is sculptural, painted or of some other sort, (which our architects make a primary aim) it is a secondary phenomenon, and it is firmly suppressed; he does not allow the slightest deviation from this principle . . . His house is a profoundly structured creation, a Whole which breathes a new beauty, which is elegantly expressed, and yet which is discreetly fitted to its purpose, for those whom it serves . . . on the path beaten out by Behrens, we can be free, we can come of age.[9]

Karl Scheffler, the critic, who saw much of Behrens about this time (and who was a pioneer of informed architectural criticism in the popular press, later editor of *Kunst und Künstler*) wrote in a special issue of *Dekorative Kunst* devoted to the Behrens house:

The sensibility which strives to experience life musically can only tolerate broad, harmonic groundnotes; only simple, full chords, in a self-created environment. Behrens' art does not wish to arouse transient, slight pleasures, nor shall it act as reins, whip or spurs to the will. But where there are folk with 'relaxed muscles and untrammelled will', who can sense, with smiling awareness, the power of melody, for them this agreeable work will be the sustained organ-tone.[10]

24

Much later, Scheffler wrote of Behrens in rather more sceptical terms that 'self-stylization had become second nature to him'. For the next few years, though, the theme of rather vaguely focused exalted enthusiasm remained central to the art of Peter Behrens. In 1905, Heinrich Pudor wrote that it was said of Behrens that he was 'neither chiefly a painter, nor an architect, nor a designer, but rather an artist of "Life" ("*Lebenskünstler*")'. He had built a house 'which bore the stamp of the owner's personality on it'. As (at the time he was writing) its artist and master now dwelt in Düsseldorf, it should not be used by others, but rather kept as it was when he lived there, 'one of a coming species'; it should be preserved as '. . . a museum of the muses, as a Behrens-Museum, or simply as the house of an artist, or, even more simply, as the house of one of those that were to come.'[11]

Notes

1. Harry Graf Kessler, *Geschichter und Zeiten: Erinnerungen*, Berlin, 1935, p219. The other remark is from Alfred Lichtwark's *Briefe*, 2 vols, Hamburg, G. Westermann, 1923, p452.
2. This is taken from a collection of essays edited by Alexander Koch entitled *Grossherzog Ernst Ludwig und die Ausstellung der Künstlerkolonie in Darmstadt von Mai bis Oktober 1901*, Darmstadt, 1901, p9. It has recently been reprinted by the Verlag zur Megede, Darmstadt, 1979.
3. See the essay by Annette Wolde, 'Der ökonomische Hintergrund der Künstlerkolonie', *Ein DDK*, op. cit. below (4).
4. Much of the information and the quotations cited in this chapter are drawn from the essays by various authors in the five-volume catalogue *Ein Dokument deutscher Kunst*, Darmstadt, Eduard Roether Verlag, 1976. This was the catalogue of the exhibition of that title held in Darmstadt (1976–77) as a review and a reconstruction in part of the original event. Much other material in this and the next chapter comes from the invaluable study by Hans-Ulrich Simon, *Sezessionismus*, Stuttgart, J. B. Metzler and Karl Ernst Poeschel, 1976; especially from chapter 8, '*Komparation mit "Fakten": Darmstadt, 1901*', pp137–72.
5. Annette Wolde, op. cit.
6. P. Morton Shand, 'Scenario for a Human Drama, Part III: Peter Behrens', *The Architectural Review*, September 1934, pp83–6.
7. Peter Behrens, *Haus Peter Behrens*, Darmstadt, *Die Ausstellung der Künstlerkolonie*, 1901. A copy of this now rare brochure is in the Klingspor Museum, Offenbach.
8. Fritz von Ostini, '*Deutsche Kunstrundreise 1901*', *Jugend VI*, 1901, No. 30, p493. Quoted in *Sezessionismus* op. cit. (p161) as follows:
   Auch der innere, seelische Zweck der Stiegen
   Er blieb' Dir noch heut' und für immer verschwiegen,
   Hätt' nicht im Tone milden Belehrens,
   Dich aufgeklärt Herr Peter Behrens!

9. Felix Commichau, *'Die Aussen-Architektur'*, *Grossherzog Ernst Ludwig* op. cit., pp90, 92, 98. Quoted in *Sezessionismus*.

10. Karl Scheffler, *'Das Haus Behrens'*, *Dekorative Kunst*, Jr. V, No. 1, Special number, Oct 1901.

11. Heinrich Pudor, *Die Gegenwart* 67–68, 1905, p295.

Behrens' House, Darmstadt, 1901

3 The Theatre and Exhibition in Darmstadt

At this time, Behrens' enthusiasm for the theatre was strongly stimulated, perhaps by his contact with Georg Fuchs, and certainly by his renewed friendship with the poet and dramatist Richard Dehmel, whom he had met in Munich, and whose woodcut portrait he had prepared for the first edition of Dehmel's *Selected Poems*.[1] His discussions with Dehmel, a national figure of the *Neuromantik*, about the theatre had a strong influence on Behrens' first major essay, a booklet entitled *Feste des Lebens und der Kunst: Ein Betrachtung des Theaters als höchsten Kultursymbols* (Celebrations of Life and Art: a consideration of the Theatre as the highest symbol of a culture). The title closely echoes Fuch's article *'Die Schaubühne: Ein Fest des Lebens'* ('The Stage: a festival of Life') and Dehmel's *'Eine Lebensmesse'* ('A Mass of Life') which appeared in the *Selected Poems*.

Written in June 1900, Behrens' twenty-five-page booklet was designed with scrupulous care. The layout and the decorations were closely related, and he employed a bold sans-serif type for the cover, an unusual step for the period.

The little book, dedicated to the artists' colony, is both a description of an ideal festival theatre (which Behrens obviously hoped might be commissioned by someone), a discussion of realism and stylization in stagecraft, and a cloudily rhetorical statement of his vision of life as a kind of artistic ritual; of the theatre as a complementary celebration of life. He used the present tense throughout, giving the statement the flavour of an incantation.

The theatre was to be high up on the side of a mountain, above a valley. It would be brightly coloured, 'as if to say, my walls have no need of sunshine!' It was to have columns hung with garlands, and seven masts bearing long white banners. From the highest points, trumpeters in glowing costumes would sound long drawn-out calls, far over the land and the forests. The great doors would open slowly, to admit the participants into a high auditorium painted in darker colours than the exterior. In an atmosphere created by colour, the sound of an organ, violins and trumpets, the spectator would be entranced. All trivial, sad or hateful thoughts would fall away, and the Play of Life would begin: 'We ourselves perform it, the beautiful drama of our solemn joy!'

The sort of plays he envisaged for this theatre would unite music and the dance, speech and movement. Tragedy would be avoided. The *Festhaus* would be cheerful, but the titillation of facetious humour would also be eschewed. Shakespearian humour, he argued mysteriously, does not make us laugh; in essence, it is serious.

There would be no scenery. The time and place of the action in a play is, he wrote, already instinct in the script. Much of the action would take place in the form of groupings and movements in relief, parallel to the proscenium. The proscenium would, incidentally, be architecturally part of the auditorium, in such a way as to effect the minimum division between the audience and the actors: 'We do not wish to separate ourselves from our art'.

The actor would speak in a rhythmical fashion; his every movement, every step would be beautiful: he would be a 'Master of the Dance'. 'The actor masters his role, he concentrates it, until all is Pathos and Pose'. There would be no set conventional times for theatrical performances; during the day, the sun would stream into the theatre; at night, artificial light would give generalized lighting, not spotlight effects. During the long intervals the audience would stay in the auditorium, or go out onto a terrace where they would look out over the hills and dales, or down on the city with its bustling activity.

There are no illustrations in the booklet *Feste*, but a plan appeared with an article he wrote for *Die Rheinlande* in January 1901.[2] This article outlined a proposal for staging Richard Dehmel's *'Eine Lebensmesse'*; one illustration shows the ground-plan of his Festival theatre; another is a detailed drawing

'Feste des Lebens und der Kunst', 1900: Dedication page.

of its stage, indicating the massing and positioning of the characters in Dehmel's play. From these plans, and from the description in *Feste*, we can get some idea of its appearance. It was to have been a circular, domed building, with four entrances at the cardinal points of the compass: the south, or main entrance ('The Portal of the Sun'); the east ('The Morning Star'); the west ('The Evening Star') were for the audience or participants.

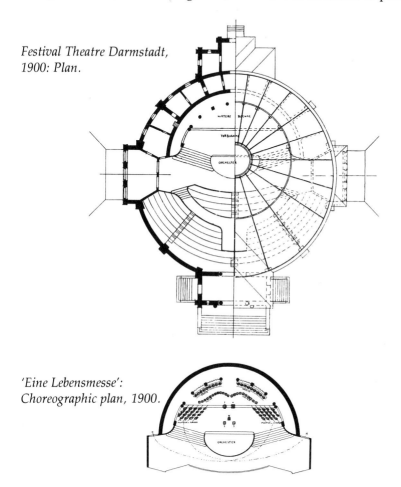

Festival Theatre Darmstadt, 1900: Plan.

'Eine Lebensmesse': *Choreographic plan, 1900.*

The north porch ('Of the Moon') was for the performers. Inside, there was a sunken orchestra pit virtually in the centre. On either side of the orchestra, broad, shallow steps gave access to the semi-circular stage which occupied more or less half the interior. Behind the stage, a semi-circular wall with a single central opening formed a kind of cyclorama; a little in front of it was a permanent setting of columns and pillars. The other half of the interior was filled with semi-circular tiers of seating. Between the stage and the seating was a flat processional way on the east-west axis.

As there are no elevations, it is tempting to visualize this building in the forms evoked by the then well-known illustrator and eccentric friend of Dehmel, Hugo Höppener or 'Fidus'. Höppener, a prominent advocate of *Lebensreform* (a movement involving nudism, dress reform, handcraftsmanship, garden city planning, Nordic folklore and other issues) had published drawings and plans of a number of visionary ritual buildings, including a fantastic *Tempel der Erde* in 1895.[3] It is also interesting to compare the plans with those of the many theatres-in-the round that have been subsequently designed and built.[4]

The last paragraph of *Feste* echoes the opening paragraph, rounding off the total effect of the statement as a sort of incantation. It ends, 'We though are fortunate, and delight that we stand at a time when once more a powerful will is alive, and faith in beauty'.

Behrens as director

In his article in *Die Rheinlande*, Behrens said that Dehmel's *'Lebensmesse'* was the first sign of the sort of theatre he believed in.

If the drama has developed from religious cults, then I see a great sign for the evolving theatre style in the fact that once more poets live who can give us and our time the forms for a Cult of Life. We will build the house from its foundations. Dehmel's *'Lebensmesse'* is a foundation stone, solemnly shaped.

It was the first creation of the new style of theatre. It contained 'no tragic conflict'; no 'plausible action' aroused emotions.

The dramatic effect of this poetic composition rests in the general rhythm of Life itself, in the incommunicable expression of Fate through elemental situations; in the harmonic interweaving of metaphoric lines of life; in short, in form: experienced and imagined form, as might be seen by a painter.

No content might be found in it, but a kind of abstraction, 'a symbol which penetrates the soul through the form of Art'.[5]

An idea of the kind of setting Behrens might have created for this or a similar production was given in an earlier essay (his first ever published), 'Stage Decoration', 1901. In this he wrote:

The décor should be stylized to the point that it is nearly or wholly transmuted into ornament, so that the whole atmosphere of the performance is to be found in colour and line. The painting should present nothing naturalistic, but rather be a beautiful, distinctive background, before which beautiful people in splendid draperies move elegantly and speak beautiful dialogue. The costumes of the chorus and supernumaries are to be used for colouristic effect . . .[6]

In his *Rheinlande* article, Behrens described the choreography of *'Eine Lebensmesse'* with the aid of the stage diagram referred to above. *'Eine Lebensmesse'* is a kind of short oratorio. It is spoken by a chorus of Elders, a chorus of Mothers, a chorus of Fathers and a chorus of Children. Individual parts are spoken by a Maiden; a Hero; an Orphan or Waif and Two Strangers. It is a secular hymn to mankind, in which these different types comment on their rôle in life and life's vicissitudes. There is next to no development or plot, although the Strangers do take the Orphan to themselves for protection during the action.

Behrens' choreography does not really amount to very much more than a rather wooden and pedestrian grouping of the cast, and a few simple movements. The chorus of Mothers with their children remain in two equal groups on either side of the stage as a symbol of eternal life. Their movements are limited to where they are standing. In a row in front of the semi-circle of columns, with a central space between them, stand the two halves of the chorus of Elders. A line of Fathers, in plan a cupid's bow shape, is ranged across the middle of the stage. In the centre of the stage, the principal soloists arrive in the order set down in Dehmel's poem; they remain in place until the end of the piece, so that a relief tableau is built up.

Behrens' main innovation in the delivery of the text was to single out some Elders from the chorus of Elders, two Chiefs from the chorus of Fathers, and two Spokeswomen from the chorus of Mothers. These would lead with parts of the verse, followed by the full chorus, in each case, rather like a part-song. After each declamation, these leading figures would melt back into their chorus, which in the case of the Elders was described as being 'a variegated blue border to the two wings of the back of the stage'. Their movements would not be 'naturalistic', but, possessing 'a life of their own', would be 'interpretations of forms of spiritual strength'.

Behrens also introduced a *Nachspiel* or finale by which the final tableau was dispersed. The actors 'leave the stage in an arranged dance, and with beautiful steps', befitting the rôle of the actor in Behrens' eyes as 'a priest of words, beautiful demeanour and the dance'. His drawing shows the path to be taken by the chorus of Mothers and Children, leaving the stage down the steps on either side of the orchestra and crossing each other in front of the audience, to exit on the opposite side. Behrens expressed the belief that the production would induce such a spiritual feeling in the audience that they would be reluctant to leave the theatre.[7]

In his plans for the theatre, Behrens was one of the pioneers, alongside Georg Fuchs, of the movement for theatre reform in Germany, which laid the ground for the tremendous success of Gordon Craig and Max Reinhardt a few years later. In his theories about stage production, Behrens was deriving a great deal from Dehmel himself, and Dehmel,[8] who was one of the earliest admirers of Nietzsche, was also receptive to the influential studies of the culture and society of ancient Greece written by Nietzsche's colleague at Basle, Jacob Burckhardt. It was from these two authors that many of Behrens' lasting views on classicism were ultimately derived.[9]

'The Sign': the opening of the Exhibition, 15 May, 1901

Behrens hoped that *'Eine Lebensmesse'* would be mounted by the Darmstadt

'Das Zeichen': Opening ceremony of the Künstlerkolonie, Darmstadt, 15 May 1901.

Künstlerkolonie, but in the event the plan came to nothing. Instead, his first practical experience of stage production came with the opening ceremony of the exhibition *Ein Dokument Deutscher Kunst*. This ceremony, in front of the *Ernst Ludwig Haus*, took the form of a festival performance of Georg Fuchs' *Das Zeichen* (The Sign). Fuchs had written a play for the Foundation-stone laying ceremony of that building, which contained workshops for the artists, reception rooms, a music room, and the apartments of Huber and Bürck.[10] The new work, *Das Zeichen*, included music by Willem de Haan, and was jointly presented by Behrens, Fuchs and de Haan.

The Sign was a crystal, carried by a *Verkünder*, a messenger, who appeared with the words, 'For you a new life begins . . .' His message was received by a chorus wearing long, costly robes, and bearing crowns on their heads. They moved in a rhythmic way; from them two soloists, a Man and a Woman detached themselves for the duration of their declamations. The effect, as the *Verkünder* and chorus were massed on the steps, was, according to Fuchs, that all the spectators (he estimated them to be 10,000) standing below were gripped by the same emotion. They were at one with the Messenger and those above, who had expressed in song the sacred wish of all. Their ambition, together, had been the *unio mystica* of the whole town, from Grand Duke to manual labourer. Wilhelm Schäfer, however, complained of the presence of 'too many simply curious townspeople of Darmstadt, and too few art-lovers from the whole Country.'

The Exhibition

When the *Grossherzog*, his wife and the Court retired from the scene at the end of this *Festspiel*, the exhibition was officially open to the public. It was to remain open until 15 October. It comprised the Ernst Ludwig Haus itself, with the artists' studios on view, the apartments of Huber and Bürck, and an exhibition of work by Huber, Bürck and Bosselt; the houses of Christiansen and Olbrich, neither of which were ready in time for the opening; the larger Glückert house, containing a permanent exhibition of furniture produced by the Darmstadt Glückert factory (this also opened late); the small Glückert house, initially planned for Bosselt, who decided that he could not afford it, (the manufacturer Glückert took it for his home instead); the Keller house, in which there was an exhibition of applied art produced by Darmstadt firms for sale or for orders; the house of Dieters, the secretary of the exhibition, and of course the Behrens house. Provisional buildings included a main entrance in the form of a canopy slung between two towers, making a sort of triumphal arch, a large building for graphic art, a *Spielhaus* (playhouse), a conservatory, an orchestra pavilion, restaurant pavilions, a postcard stand and so on. All the buildings other than the Behrens house were by Olbrich. Season tickets were 20 marks, for families 25–8 marks. There were daily concerts by the new Philharmonic Orchestra from Vienna, there were Garden and Folk festivals, and at night, dances, fireworks, illuminations (by Christiansen), and a tombola at which objects by the Darmstadt 'Seven' could be won.

At the Playhouse, there was a series of *Darmstädter Spiele*, in which theatrical experiments of a kind considered impossible on the commercial stage were mounted. Olbrich and Behrens were initially to be responsible for these productions, at alternate periods. Both had their circle of literary friends, and Behrens at first had some promising response from writers associated with the *Insel* circle in Munich—Schröder, Bierbaum, Hugo von Hofmannsthal and Dehmel. Olbrich brought in Wilhelm Holzamer from Vienna, and gave him the first period of direction of the stage. Holzamer's *Weihespiele* which inaugurated the season, were not a success. They appear to have consisted of a series of *tableaux* and fragments that aimed at the creation of 'mood-pictures'. In one, for example, a spectral figure emerged enigmatically from the darkened stage and left, through the audience, by way of the auditorium. The audiences also melted away from these 'mystical-symbolic mood scenes', finding even the spoken verse incomprehensible. The most successful events, towards the end of the season, appear to have been Wolzogen's *Überbrettl*, a sort of literary cabaret, very much more lighthearted and entertaining in tone. Songs and poems by Liliencron, Bierbaum, Wolzogen and others formed the basis of dances, little pantomimes and shadow plays. Although criticized by some in Darmstadt as too frivolous, or even risqué, the general feeling was that they were 'not uninteresting' and inoffensive. In this climate nothing came of Behrens' grander ambitions, and Dehmel's '*Lebensmesse*' was not staged. Later in his career, in Mannheim, in Cologne and in Berlin, he made further attempts, in vain, to produce it.

The Überdokument

In July, the *Darmstädter Zeitung* announced the intention of the artists to mount a 'completely new exhibition . . . in the style that anyone might have had presented to them, had they only read certain newspaper reports'. The artists wished 'to present an opening ceremony in front of an invited audience, likewise in the light of a certain Press'.

This extraordinary exhibition, parodying the main one, was opened at the end of August. It was set out on the Mathildenhöhe on the site where today the Exhibition Building and Olbrich's *Hochzeitsturm* stand. This exhibition, dubbed the *Überdokument* (a play on the title *Ein Dokument*, attaching the prefix '*über*' to make a word reminiscent of the word *Überbrettl*—a variety entertainment) was devised by the Seven themselves. It included miniature papier-mâché and wood replicas, in caricature, of the main buildings and the houses; a theatre; a shooting gallery at which the public could take pot shots at images of the principal critics of the Darmstadt experiment, and other side-shows. The *Überdokument* opened with a burlesque ceremony including a fancy-dress parade guying *Reformkleidung* (dress-reform) and Art Nouveau hair styles. An *Über-Haupt-Katalog* was published, as a parody of the *Hauptkatalog* of the main exhibition. This contained, among other things, a pastiche of the opening ceremony, *Das Zeichen*, rendered in gross Bavarian dialect. There were amusing caricatures of the houses. Behrens' house is shown here as an extremely wobbly affair bearing the motto '*Fest steh' mein Haus im Sturmgebraus!*' ('Stand fast, my house, in the tumult of the storm!') and Behrens' statements concerning his

Caricature of Behrens' house (cartoonist unnamed), from Der Überdokument, 1901.

house are parodied in the text. The 'logical interplay of an artistic sensibility, united with our new technical advances and with new materials', for example, becomes '. . . the angle at which the supporting props are leaning against the house walls is exactly calculated. Both are of genuine materials, especially the logical development of the props'.

The aim of this whole exercise was presumably to take the wind out of the sails of the critics of the exhibition by anticipating their criticism and exaggerating it to make it look ridiculous. It might also have been offered as a little light relief to the elevated tone of the official literature put out by the colony, in the manner of an end-of-term revue put on by the students of a college. It is not surprising, however, that many people were bewildered by this rather elephantine self-parody and didn't know how to take it. In the eyes of some visitors, the *Überdokument* was a lapse in taste that compounded the faults of the *Dokument* itself. Harry Graf Kessler visited the exhibition at this time, in the company of Henry van de Velde. 'We are both thoroughly disgusted, particularly at this tasteless self-mockery'. According to Kessler, Van de Velde was extremely hostile to the *Dokument* as a whole:

Van de Velde was . . . at first stupefied, and then collected himself and said . . . 'What these people have done there is exactly the opposite of that we wish to do . . . a sense of the organic is lacking, any respect for the use of materials . . . [and following a second visit on 2 September] . . . He was again very indignant: 'No, I'm repelled. I won't use ornament any more for two years. I'm glad to have seen it. One sees what not to do. I will become even simpler, I will seek nothing but form.'[12]

There was indeed a good deal of adverse criticism, and not all from the philistines. It was perhaps inevitable that there would be a reaction against the fulsome propaganda that had been put out for nearly a year in advance of the exhibition; this rebounded upon itself to some degree, and fostered disappointment. There was also trouble with a Press looking for sensations and easy targets for fun. The circle around Koch, perhaps the instigators of the whole scheme, felt that no great victory over historicism had been achieved. Others, however, did find it a positive virtue that no 'Style' could, in the historical sense, be found anywhere in the exhibition. Lichtwark damned with faint praise 'one of the most amusing experiments of our time . . .' Meier-Graefe spoke of 'the fiasco of the Darmstadt exhibition'. Michael Georg Conrad shared the view of Lichtwark, that it mostly only interested 'the well-to-do Darmstadt and Frankfurt middle classes'. He wrote:

In these rooms with their fairy-tale colours and magic-lantern quality, life is a holiday. It is more than a life among beauty—it is a life apart. Here one withdraws to recover from bitter confinement and hard struggles. Here one is a guest of the Olympian gods. For striving, care-worn folk this is no home for everyday life. Here, modern man can only pause fleetingly for the favour of a glimpse and a deep inward breath. Should he stay, he will degenerate into sick sensuality, living in a fool's paradise. Also—as a working artists' community—this place, select and high-minded, could be recommended for very young and very beautiful honeymooners.

Many indeed saw the houses as 'dwellings for a really small, exclusive class of people' and 'impractical for most people'. More seriously, some thought that the whole exhibition had 'a crazy, un-German appearance', and some attacks, anticipating the Nazi response to the *Weissenhof Siedlung* in Stuttgart a quarter of a century later and using similar terminology, saw 'a stylistic revival on an Asiatic pattern', and made mock of 'Cairo in Berlin', 'a mixture of Vienna and Tunis'.

A good deal of the criticism distinguished between the contributions of Olbrich and Behrens, and praise of one tended to imply criticism of the other. The relationship between Behrens and Olbrich deteriorated during the period and to some extent they acquired rival followings. To some, Behrens' house stood out on the Mathildenhöhe for its stiffness and outward restraint. Schäfer, for example, saw a 'careful construction, geometric in its logic' and he was relieved to find 'none of the appalling modern garter stripes' on it, or 'blinding colour-symphonies' which he obviously detested in the Art Nouveau elements of Olbrich's houses. Some wrote, concerning Olbrich and Behrens, of the opposition of constructive principles versus decoration (although construction is in reality no more logically expressed in Behrens' house than in those of Olbrich); rationality compared with vitality, the opposition of the northern temperament against the southern, the native of Hamburg compared with the Viennese.

Alfred Lichtwark decided on balance that Olbrich's own house was 'all in all, the least extravagant' of the Mathildenhöhe buildings.

Notes

For further discussion of Behrens and the theatre, see Anderson op. cit. and Simon op. cit.; also Jutta Boehe, *Theater und Jugendstil-Feste des Lebens und der Kunst* and *Darmstädter Spiele 1901* in G. Bott (Ed.), *Von Morris zum Bauhaus, Eine Kunst gegründet auf Einfachkeit*, Hanau, Peters, 1977.

1. In Richard Dehmel, *Ausgewählte Gedichte*, Berlin, Schuster und Loeffler, 1902. The woodcut was also available in a limited edition of 100. Dehmel appears younger than in the 1903 woodcut. *'Eine Lebensmesse'*, first published in 1898, was included in this selection.

2. *Die Rheinlande* I, Jan 1901, No. 1, vol 4. (Special number on the Darmstadt *Künstlerkolonie*, pp28–40.)

3. See Janos Frecot, Johann Friedrich Geist and Diethart Kerbs, *Fidus 1868–1948*, Munich, Rogner & Bernhard, 1972, pp233–47.

4. It is possible that Behrens was inspired by Friedrich Gilly's *Essai sur la construction d'un théâtre à la manière des théâtres grecs et romains*, 1797. On this see Julius Posener, *Berlin auf dem Wege zu einer neuen Architektur: Der Zeitalter Wilhelms II, 1890–1918*, Munich, Prestel, 1979.

5. These two quotations come from *Die Rheinlande* I, Jan 1901, and from Behrens' article '*Die Dekoration der Bühne*', *Das literarische Echo*, Yr. 2, No. 17, pp1213–15.

6. Peter Behrens, '*Die Dekoration der Bühne*', *Deutsche Kunst und Dekoration*, July 1900, vol VI, pp401–5.

7. The setting, with its screen of columns, arch and flight of steps down to the auditorium, is different in plan, but similar in stage-craft to that of Walter Crane's 'Beauty's Awakening, A Masque of Winter and of Spring' which was performed at the Guildhall, London on 28 June 1899. It was illustrated in the Summer Number of the *Studio* in 1899 and Behrens could easily have seen a copy. This masque was surely as silly in an English way as Behrens' and Dehmel's schemes were in a German way.

8. Dehmel recognized his hand in Behrens' tract. See his letters to G. Kühl (2.2.01) and to Johannes Schaf (6.12.02). Dehmel, *Ausgewählte Briefe 1883–1902* op. cit.

9. Janet Leeper in her short article, 'Peter Behrens and the Theatre', *The Architectural Review*, vol 144, pp138–9, August 1968, stresses the pioneer role of Behrens and Fuchs along with the Swiss Adolf Appia, whose *Die Musik und die Inszenierung*, Munich, Bruckmann, was well known to them, in the reform of the German theatre. She discusses Behrens' staging of Hartleben's *Diogenes* in the *Parkhaus*, Hagen, in 1909—not long after Hartleben's death. See also Herta Hesse-Frielinghaus et al, *Karl Ernst Osthaus, Leben und Werk*, Recklinghausen, Bongers, 1971, for many references to this, the sole theatrical event Behrens was able to design and direct.

10. Published in *Deutsche Kunst und Dekoration*, April–September 1900, pp357–65. A colour reproduction of Fuchs' *Zur Weihe des Grundsteins* (a little address for the foundation stone laying ceremony) with its decorations by Behrens, is illustrated in *Ein Dokument Deutscher Kunst*, 1976, vol 5, p211.

11. Wilhelm Schäfer, *Ein Dokument Deutscher Kunst, Die Rheinlande*, June 1901, pp38–40.

12. Harry Graf Kessler, quoted by Van de Velde in his *Geschichte meines Lebens*, Munich, 1962, p488. Their visit was between 31 August and 2 September.

4 Behrens' Lettering and Typography

Behrens' earliest published attempts at lettering appear to have been his decorative title-headings (*Kopfleiste*) for the fifth volume (1899) of *Deutsche Kunst und Dekoration*. The thin, jaunty letters are typical of those associated with Art Nouveau graphic art and are harmoniously fitted into their decorative, floral frames. The heading for the review of the Munich Arts and Crafts exhibition at the *Glaspalast* (in which he himself exhibited work) is typical. These first letters follow the success of his typographical ornament and layout for Otto Julius Bierbaum's *Kalenderbuch* of 1898, '*Der Bunte Vogel*'. He also drew the titles of his wood-cuts: a sort of Roman for the 'Bismarck' of 1899, and sans-serif block letters fitting into squares for the Hartleben and Dehmel portraits.

Decorative heading from Deutsche Kunst und Dekoration, 1899.

His first printing type was a kind of *Deutsche Fraktur* or black letter script, best known as Behrens-Schrift. A specimen appeared with an introduction, initial letters and decorative details in October 1902, published by the *Rudhard'sche Giesserei* of Offenbach-am-Main. This was the typefoundry of the Klingspor brothers, a little later known as the *Schriftgiesserei Gebrüder Klingspor*. It appears that the publisher Eugen Diederichs put Behrens in touch with the Klingspor brothers. On 17 May 1900, Behrens wrote to Diederichs enclosing a copy of the *Festschrift* containing Georg Fuch's *Festspiel* for the Darmstadt colony. Behrens had designed the decorative title heading. He also called attention to his own essay on stage design. He then went on to discuss his struggle to design a typeface:

I've experienced the most depressing things with my type, which is now ready. All those who have an opinion to air on matters of typography naturally find it 'outstanding', but would like to have this or that altered. And if I gave in on it, they would eliminate everything that is really individual in it, until it is a type just like all the rest. No one, not even Jessen, who will go such a long way with me, will grasp that it isn't a matter of reconstructing a good old type face, but to find a new one, adapted to our present-day feelings and style. If one reflects that in its own day people could get accustomed to rococo flourishes of the 'black letter', it is unbelievable that they can't get used to simplicity and readability. The script on Georg Fuchs' title page in the *Festschrift* won't give you any real idea of the type. That title is from a still unfinished stage of development . . . On the advice of a know-all who has some influence on my typefounder, I let myself be persuaded to prepare a second, more rounded, open script, and to employ the first one as a bold type for paragraph headings (used in the same way I employed the gothic type in the report). The result: the fellow will only have my flowing script and I have come to the point where my heart sinks right down, and I see the weak and enfeebled version used, the one which doesn't mean as much to me. I would dearly like the founder (who is, after all, nothing more than a peasant in Stuttgart) to have neither if he won't take both, and for me to bide my time. Only it's a delicate question, for the work to depend on such a matter. What do you think? Do you perhaps know a founder who has eyes for the coming style of our time? I'd be most grateful if you could revive your earlier interest in my affairs enough to drop me a few lines . . .[1]

Diederich's advice was presumably to try the Klingspor brothers. They had pioneered the renaissance of fine printing in Germany and had already issued a printing type by Behrens' friend of his Hamburg and Munich days, Otto Eckmann. Eckmann's type had appeared in 1900 and had been a sensational success. Designed with a brush and influenced by Japanese prints, it was closely integrated with the floral ornamentation designed in conjunction with it. Its success followed that of his famous title, similar in style, for the illustrated weekly *Die Woche*. About it, Behrens wrote:

If you ask me about Eckmann's type, and would like to know my real opinion of it, I must say that I find it very readable (which is something to be valued) but not beautiful, because of the basic principle of the thing. It is a type that is developed from the brushstroke. This, in its pure form, is beautiful in Chinese and Japanese script; but considered from *our* form-tradition, it is impossible to banish the association it has with a striking newspaper advertisement. I am of the opinion, rather, that we need a really serious style of type for really serious books. Then we will bring this beautiful style into our everyday life, and even our newspapers will be of a different stamp.[2]

Although it was, like Eckmann's, a fusion of Roman and Gothic lettering, Behrens-Schrift was based on pen lettering. It is austere and carefully proportioned, not floral in inspiration, but based on the Gothic hand used in manuscripts. Fritz Ehmcke (the graphic designer whom Behrens later called to work with him in Düsseldorf) compared it with a steel framework. The crossbars of the capitals A, E, F, G and H, for example, are in line with the tops of the lower case letters. The capitals F, J, L, M, P and W and the lower case g, p and s are closest to the old traditional Fraktur type, then still in common use. All rounded forms are made angular, and the letters are tall and narrow.

Behrens-Schrift, 1902: (above) Behrens' original calligraphy; (below) the typeface.

Behrens wrote an introductory note '*Von der Entwicklung der Schrift*' ('On the evolution of the type'). This gives some historical analysis of the development of letter forms, and a discussion of his own script:

A new typeface can only develop organically and almost unnoticeably from a tradition, and only in harmony with the new spiritual and material stuff of the entire epoch. For the precise form of my type I took the technical principle of gothic script, the stroke of the quill pen. Also, in order to achieve an even more German character, gothic letters were a decisive influence on me for the proportions, the height and width of the letters and the thickness of the strokes. A character that holds together well, in such a way that all superfluities might be eliminated, so that the constructional principle of the diagonally held pen might be clearly expressed, was what I sought.

He also made an interesting statement on the reading qualities of a good typeface or handwritten letter:

One takes in a script, when reading properly, as one sees the flight of a bird or the gallop of a horse. Both are pleasant, graceful phenomena, without remarking the shapes of individual limbs of the animal, or a momentary position. It is the line as a whole, and this is fundamentally the same in writing.

Behrens own handwriting was, incidentally, very beautiful—strong, bold, rhythmical and easily read.

Behrens' second typeface, the Kursiv, was designed during the years 1906–07. This, also cut and published by the Klingspor brothers, is an italic, with an elegant, flowing character strongly akin to the Behrens-Schrift, but clearly abandoning the attempt to fuse the old-fashioned black letter with the Roman. It is based on early romanesque German scripts, and differs from Behrens-Schrift in having softer, more curved forms throughout. It is carefully proportioned and without superfluous flourishes or arbitrary thickenings. There are boldly ascending strokes in the capital A, F, H and M; a long, strongly curved lower case s and a similar g, which gives lines of Kursiv type an animated, rhythmical swing. The typographical ornament accompanying the Kursiv is delightful. Behrens' view of ornament at this point was that it should be impersonal and abstract. For the Kursiv the designs were of spirals and light geometrical patterns, derived from Greek pottery. He was using the same sort of patterns as decoration on his architecture during this period.

The Kursiv appeared in 1907, after Behrens had held two courses on lettering and typography at the School of Arts and Crafts in Düsseldorf, under the auspices of the Prussian Ministry for Trade and Industry. These courses, for teachers in technical and design colleges, were taught by Behrens, Ehmcke and Anna Simons. For the first course, in 1906, Behrens tried to get Edward Johnston to come from England (on the advice of Hermann Muthesius and Harry Graf Kessler), but in the event his German pupil Anna Simons came instead. She also participated in the second Düsseldorf *Schriftkursus* in July–August 1907, shortly before Behrens left to begin his work with the AEG. A further course was held in the summer of 1909, in Neubabelsberg in Berlin, where Behrens was then living.[3]

Anna Simons translated Johnston's *Writing, Illuminating and Lettering* into German, and collaborated with Behrens in detailing the monumental inscription '*Dem Deutschen Volke*' ('Of the German people') for the pediment of Paul Wallot's Reichstag building. Initially the Kaiser forbade the installation of the bronze letters of this democratic inscription on the building he contemptuously dismissed as 'the gossip shop'. Pressure from left-wing politicians is believed to have further hardened the attitude of the Kaiser, who in any case thought the building to be 'the height of tastelessness'. Although Behrens and Fräulein Simons designed the inscription in 1909, it was not until 1917 that the then Chancellor, Theobald von Bethmann Holl-

Behrens Kursiv und Schmuck, 1907.

weg persuaded the Kaiser to agree to its addition. Although damaged in the fire of 1933 and the bombardment of Berlin, the inscription survived, and proudly stands, restored, over the renovated portico of the Reichstag.[4]

Behrens paid tribute to Anna Simons for her 'many-sided stimulation', her knowledge of antique and medieval techniques of lettering, and her familiarity with the English school of calligraphy stemming from Morris, Johnston and others.

Friedrich der Große

B C D E H
I K L S U

ZUR AUFKLÄRUNG

Behrens Mediäval (top), 1914 and Antiqua initials and capitals, 1908.

The Reichstag by Paul Wallot, 1882–94. Inscription by Peter Behrens and Anna Simons, 1909.

43

Behrens' next type was his Antiqua, which he first used for the catalogue he prepared for the *Deutsche Schiffbauausstellung* (The Shipbuilding Exhibition of 1908, Berlin), for which he designed the AEG Pavilion.

Behrens-Antiqua is a Roman alphabet. It differs from Morris's 'Golden Type' or Emery Walker's 'Doves' in being inspired by uncial letters of the fifth century—a parallel with Behrens' contemporary enthusiasm for

Beßrens-Kurſiv

Geſeßlich geſchüßt!

1509   Text · 20 Punkte   Saß etwa 9 Kilo

Fr. Schiller: Es gibt im Menschenleben Augenblicke, wo er dem Weltgeiſt näher iſt als ſonſt, und eine Frage frei hat an das Schickſal.

1510   Doppelmittel · 28 Punkte   Saß etwa 11 Kilo

Notes and Queries on Electrotyping and 12345 Stereotyping Machines 67890

1511   3 Cicero · 36 Punkte   Saß etwa 14 Kilo

Deutſches Kunſtgewerbe auf der Weltausſtellung St. Louis

1512   4 Cicero · 48 Punkte   Saß etwa 20 Kilo

Assemblée Nationale 23. Janvier 1809

Gebr. Klingspor in Offenbach am Main

Behrens Kursiv, 1907.

44

Carolingian and early Romanesque architecture, which he used as a direct source of inspiration for his own work. A precedent for the Antiqua may be found in the lettering of his poster for the *Deutsche Jahrhundertausstellung* (The German Centennial Exhibition) in Berlin of January 1906. The lettering of this poster, although relatively clumsy, has some features that appear in Behrens-Antiqua—the heavily emphasized vertical downstrokes of the letters, the unvaried thickness of the diagonal upstrokes, and the triangular serifs. Some initials of Behrens-Antiqua had appeared before the type was published in October 1908, such as the 'D' which was used as early as 1907 for the *Rathenau-Adresse* and again for the AEG *Festschrift* which commemorated the twenty-fifth anniversary of the firm, on 14 April 1908. An initial A was printed in *Kunst und Künstler* in December 1907,[5] so many of the initials must have been designed during or before 1907. (Schauer writes that the type as a whole was essentially designed as early as 1903.[6])

The direct prototype of Behrens-Antiqua was, according to Karl Klingspor, the uncial of the *Codex Argenteus* of Upsala.[7] The uncial prototype appears especially in the capitals C, D, F, P, U and the alternative form of E. The peculiarity of the serifs projecting only to the left above and to the right below appears in ancient manuscripts; it is marked in the capitals A, H, T, K, M, N, R and U, and in the lower case letters a, h, k, l, m, n, r and u: it gives a walking movement to the lines. Up and down strokes are sharply distinguished from one another, having been made with a horizontally held broad pen. The forms so created are reminiscent of *Capitalis Quadrata* pen capitals, which look like stone-cut inscriptional lettering. The only letter to step out of the stiff rectilinear line is the Q with its long sweeping tail. The rectangular character of the script is not simply encouraged by the use of a horizontally held pen, but is a sign of the unity in Behrens' creative activity; it is the work of an architect who was constantly using squares and cubes as the basis for his designs at the same time that he was working on his typography.[8]

In the preface ('*Zum Geleit*') to the specimen brochure, the historical derivation of the type is discussed, and there is a strong emphasis, characteristic of the growing nationalism of the time, on its specifically Germanic form:

It is to be hoped that the new Behrens type, with its direct connection with the Roman of the Germanic cultural world is a further stimulation to the use of the Roman in a German spirit, approached in the right way, . . . may, in addition, a coherent German script consequently play a wider and more valuable part, may the foundations be laid to a GERMAN ANTIQUA!

The decorative embellishments that accompanied the Antiqua were very closely derived from the late Roman bronze and silver grave furnishings (buckles and so on) that were found in Austria-Hungary, and which were the subject of Alois Riegl's famous study *Die spätrömische Kunstindustrie nach Funden in Osterreich-Ungarn* (1901). There is no doubt that Behrens studied the illustrations in this book; there is, moreover, reason to suppose that he read the theoretical part of Riegl's work carefully, and applied the principles of design suggested by Riegl's analysis of pattern and style in ancient art.[9]

As Riegl related stylistic forms in art to social, religious and scientific (that is, the technical) conditions of the period he was considering, so did Behrens, who remarked in his *'Von der Entwicklung der Schrift'* of 1902, that letter forms give 'next to architecture, quite the most characteristic picture of a period, and the strongest testimonial of the spiritual progress of development of a people'. Behrens considered that he was, like an artist of the Renaissance, both serving modern needs and making manifest the forms stimulated by the most advanced scholarly enthusiasm and theory of his time. At a deeper level, he was trying, like so many German artists of his generation, to divine the artistic mode of expression which would be the healthy, natural and fruitful style of modern German culture. He overlooked, as did the others, that the individual, working self-consciously within the vast, shifting complexity of his contemporary culture, cannot establish a 'style' in the sense in which he observes it in the work of some anonymous artisan of the distant past.

He not only made direct interpretations of the engraved bronze ornamental patterns of those Balkan tribes of late antiquity, the subject of Riegl's investigations, but also, in the design of the initials for Behrens-Antiqua, made use of pattern elements drawn from the 'animal style', only without any grotesque heads or figurative detail.[10] These offered infinitely adjustable, space-filling, rhythmically curved forms making a counterpoint of light and dark tones, of solids and voids. The positive-negative qualities of his *Zierat* (decorative embellishments); the 'contrasted or opposed curves'; the 'continuous rhythmical exchange of light and dark' were all qualities analysed by Riegl. The procedure of the ancient craftsmen led, according to Riegl, to 'an equalizing of the background and the individual, detached forms'. Behrens' designs and typography attempted to relate shapes to one another in this way, and to establish all the motifs on one flat plane.

Behrens-Antiqua was often used for AEG material, and it also formed the basis of his AEG type. He developed variations on a characteristic Roman face with softer, more rounded serifs, the capital E of which has a very noticeable, elongated central stem terminating in a backward-sloping serif. An original pencil drawing for one of these variations survives, and a sketchbook page also exists which has preliminary drawings with the note 'poliphili'—an interesting reference to one of its models, the famous Renaissance book *Hypnerotomachia Poliphili*.

Behrens often drew special inscriptions or titles with different Roman faces. The title of the *AEG Zeitung* for 1 August 1906 is in a slender and elegant letter. Addresses like that to Emil Rathenau, (for the award of the *Grashof-Denkmünze* to him by the *Verein Deutscher Ingenieure*)[11] or the goodwill address from the *Berliner Elektricitäts-Werke* to the AEG on its twenty-fifth anniversary, were carried out in a mixture of Behrens-Antiqua initials and decorations, and specially drawn script and decoration.

Behrens' last type published by Klingspor was the Mediäval. This was probably begun in 1906–7, taken up again and developed between 1909 and 1913, and finally published in 1914. It is a Renaissance type, with jaunty, sloping serifs and long, projecting upper strokes on the lower case letters such as h, d and s. The downwards projecting parts of the p and g are short and tight. There is relatively little difference between the upward and downward strokes, so that it is a light, rhythmical and warm alphabet. Schauer called it the 'fair sister' of the serious, weighty Antiqua. Leitmeier[12] thought that there were traces of *Jugendstil* in the flourish of letters like the capitals C, G, J and T, and also in the lower case e and tall s. The curious triangular thickenings in the intersections of parts of these and other letters are a novelty. The double s is particularly graceful and ingenious.

Allgemeine Elektrizitäts Geſellſchaft
PROF. PETER BEHRENS
NEUBABELSBERG
Hamburg Amerika Linie

Blockletter for the AEG, 1916.

From time to time, Behrens either used or designed block or sans-serif letters. Those for his early woodcuts have been mentioned. He used a simple sans-serif for his *Feste des Lebens und der Kunst*,[13] and he devised one for the exhibition pavilion of the *Delmenhorster Linoleum Fabrik* (at Dresden in 1906) and for the related publicity material. Another was used for the AEG catalogue of 1908 for Christmas tree lights. The same sort of lettering appears in photographs of AEG showrooms in Berlin as early as 1910, applied to the glass display windows. An undated design exists in a Berlin private collection for a grotesque or sans-serif. This appears to be the design for a letter that was an AEG standard type in 1916, and used for various purposes. It is a remarkable parallel to the famous sans-serif designed in England by Edward Johnston for the London Underground. (A closely related version was popularized in the 1920s and 30s by the Monotype Corporation as Gill Sans). Johnston's sans-serif was designed, according to his daughter, in the spring of 1916, in a back bedroom in Ditchling.[14] In 1937, Johnston wrote to John Farleigh:

I might add that this particular design appears to have become of considerable historic importance (in the world of alphabets). It is in fact the foundational model of *all modern* respectable Block letters—including those painted on Roads and signs for motorists and Eric Gill's very popular sans-serif type. It seems also to have made a great impression in parts of central Europe, where I understand it has given me a reputation which my own country is too practical to recognize.

It seems as if Behrens, the follower of Johnston through Anna Simons, was in fact working in an exactly parallel direction to that of the Englishman, at the same time, and quite independently.

Notes

1. Letter from Behrens to Diederichs, 17 May 1900. Eugen Diederichs, *Selbstzeugnisse und Briefe von Zeitgenossen*, Düsseldorf and Cologne, Diederichs, 1967, pp111–13.

2. Letter from Behrens to Diederichs, 24 August 1900. Diederichs op. cit., pp114–15.

3. F. Ehmcke, A. Simons, *'In Erinnerungen an gemeinsamen Arbeit'*, *Schriften der Corona VIII*, Zürich, 1938.

4. Heinz Raack, *Das Reichstagsgebäude in Berlin*, Berlin, Gebr. Mann, Studio-Reihe, 1978, p43.

5. Karl Ernst Osthaus, 'Peter Behrens', *Kunst und Künstler* No. 3, Dec 1907, p116.

6. G. K. Schauer, *Deutsche Buchkunst 1890 bis 1960* vol 1, Hamburg, Maximilian Gesellschaft, 1963.

7. Julius Rodenberg, 'Karl Klingspor', *The Fleuron* V, 1926.

8. Other discussions of Peter Behrens' typography include Karl Klingspor, *Über Schönheit vom Schrift und Drucke*, Frankfurt, Schauer, 1949, pp21–2; Roswitha Riegger-Baurmann, *'Schrift im Jugendstil in Deutschland'*, *Jugendstil* (Ed. Jost Hermand), Darmstadt, Wissenschaftlicher Buchgesellschaft, 1971, pp248–52; Wilhelm H. Lange, *'Peter Behrens und die Schriftkunst unserer Zeit'*, *Archiv für Buchgewerbe und Gebrauchsgraphik*, No. 75, 1938, pp161–4.

9. See the important discussion of Behrens' typography in: Gabriele Heidecker, *'Das Werbe-Kunst-Stück; Ausstellungen und Läden, Schriften und Werbegraphik für die AEG'*, *Industriekultur: Peter Behrens und die AEG, 1907–1914* (Ed. Tilmann Buddensieg and Henning Rogge) Berlin, Gebr. Mann Verlag, 1979, pp167–97.

10. In a similar way he adapted motifs from the enamel elements of the *Lothar Evangeliar* book cover for his Krupp Address of 1912. This was a gift from the AEG to commemorate the 100th anniversary of Krupp's.

11. Which can be compared with the Godescalc Evangelistar (781–783) or the Evangeliar of St Gereon.

12. Hans Leitmeier, *'Die Bedeutung des Jugendstils für das deutsche Buch, und Walter Tiemanns Anteil daran'*, *Gutenberger Jahrbuch*, Mainz, 1959, p184. Also see Walter Tiemann, *Deutsche Typengestaltung seit 1900*, *Gutenberger Jahrbuch*, Mainz, 1950, p299.

13. The pamphlet was published by Diederichs. In a letter to Diederichs, 25 July 1900, Behrens wrote:

I think that it could be set in a Roman type, of a solemn, somewhat stirring kind, adapted both to the style of the article and to the object itself as a book. I would like best to closely supervise the printing here, with Winter, and to design the whole typographical layout myself.

—Eugen Diederichs, *Selbstzeugnisse und Briefe von Zeitgenossen* op. cit., p113.

14. Priscilla Johnston, *Edward Johnston*, London, Faber & Faber, 1959, p203.

Logo for the AEG, 1907.

5 The Years 1902–7

Darmstadt, 1902–3

During 1901, Behrens was concerned with several projects outside Darmstadt. These included an invitation to teach in Nürnberg. Behrens directed a course in applied art for established craftsmen, sponsored by the *Bayerisches Gewerbemuseum*. The course ran for a month in October–November, and, as a result of its success, was repeated in January–February 1902. (A third course was run in 1903 by Richard Riemerschmidt.) The object of these courses was to act as a corrective to the adoption of half-understood *Art Nouveau* mannerisms by local craftsmen, quite apart from debased versions of historical styles, and to bring them into contact with a leading artist of the new movement. Behrens was concerned to guide and criticize from the basis of principle rather than to impose a style, although it is reported that much of the work produced did in fact tend to reflect his current, Darmstadt, style. The experiment was an interesting minor episode in the development of modern art education in Germany.[1]

More important for his growing reputation was, however, his contribution to the First International Exhibition of Modern Decorative Arts (April–November 1902) in Turin. Behrens designed three interiors within the suite of galleries which represented the official German contribution, and which was co-ordinated overall by the Munich architect H. E. von Berlepsch-Valendas. The various halls, rooms and antechambers were devoted to sections illustrating the applied art and interior design of various parts of Germany–Prussia, Saxony, Bavaria and so on.

Behrens was responsible for the striking *Hamburger Vorhalle* or vestibule, for a reception room destined ultimately for the house of Ludwig Alter (also known as the *Hessisches Zimmer*) and a study for the display of the publications of Alexander Koch's firm.

The *Hamburger Vorhalle* or *Vestibül* was a rectangular room within which a massive arcade had been created. Each of the four walls was opened up with a wide arch, flat-topped, with huge voussoirs and keystones. Bracket-like cross vaults in each corner supported a flat ceiling which was pierced with a large rectangular opening, covered with a yellow opalescent glazed canopy. Each corner was formed by two parabolic arches, above which the roof was

50

(Above) Hamburger Vestibül, Turin, 1902.

(Left) Table lamp, 1902.

51

glazed blue. The whole ensemble created a pool of golden light in the middle of the room, and shafts of blue light, mysteriously hooded by the arches supporting the roof, flooding the arched corners. The grotto-like effect was enhanced by trailing plants that hung down all round the opening in the ceiling, reminiscent of the *Serapeum* of Hadrian's villa at Tivoli.

In the centre of the room was a rectangular sunken pool with rounded ends: at either end knelt two winged figures of cement. 'Noble, but somewhat stiff-winged figures, so characteristic of their author' commented the correspondent of the *Studio* magazine.[2] Behrens used a similar motif for a table lamp he designed about this time for the *Grossherzog* Ernst Ludwig.

In the centre of one wall of the *Hamburger Vestibül*, a bronze door set in a parabolic arch was hung on extraordinary hinges that formed part of a huge band of decoration across the leaves of the doors. Above this entrance was an early bronze relief by the Hamburg sculptor Ernst Barlach, dedicated to the Hamburg shipbuilding concern, Blohm und Voss. In other corner arches were bronze panels by Behrens himself, decorated with standing draped female figures. Behrens also designed the oak display cases, in one of which was displayed his monumental binding of a copy of Nietzsche's *Also Sprach Zarathustra*.

This interior was by far the most fey and Art Nouveau of Behrens' architectural works, and the most Belgian influenced of his designs, strongly resembling the Brussels interiors of Victor Horta—the Hotels Solvay, Aubecq or Dubois for example. In his review of the exhibition, L. Gmelin reported that many visitors found it too sepulchral, 'with a certain resemblance to a crypt', and that others thought that it was more like 'the sanctuary of a Vehmic Court' than the entrance to the German Gallery.[3]

The Ludwig Alter room and the Library for Koch publications were by contrast very much more restrained and rectilinear. The *Studio* critic felt that they were 'very superior' to the interiors of Behrens' Darmstadt house, and although he made it clear that he was both aware of the rivalry of Olbrich and Behrens, and that he considered Olbrich by far the best architect and decorator in Germany, he generously conceded that 'very much may yet be expected of Behrens . . . he is a sound, sincere, earnest and thoroughly reliable worker'. He unfortunately qualified his praise of Behrens ('he has lately made a very distinct advance') with the double-edged compliment '. . . simply because he has approached Olbrich the more nearly'.

Other interiors of 1902 were for a villa in Sachen am Bodensee,[4] and a dining-room for the exhibition, held in the autumn, of Modern Living Rooms at A. Wertheim's store in Berlin, the newly completed building by Alfred Messel.

This room was rectilinear, centred on a square table for four, over which hung a complicated light fitting of cubic and rectangular shades, constructed within a cage of metal rods. Max Osborn wrote of the room:

The fascination of the dining-room set up in Wertheim's in the autumn of 1902 lay in the manner in which a basic rectangular form was logically divided up into little squares and strips with a linear grid, which was extended all over, into the stencilled wall patterns, the carpet, the light fitting, the furniture and the crockery.[5]

It appears to have been an early example of the use by Behrens of a proportional grid of some kind in the design of a harmonious scheme—an approach that became central to the development of his architecture in the years to come.

Düsseldorf 1903–7

There is no doubt that Behrens became increasingly dissatisfied with the Darmstadt Künstlerkolonie during 1902. Where the architecture of the Mathildenhöhe was concerned, Olbrich still held the field (and indeed continued to contribute further important buildings to the site until his death in 1908), and of course Behrens' plans for the theatre were unrealized. (As late as 1918 Dehmel could still write with bitterness of the 'intrigues of the artist-craftsmen' which had frustrated their scheme.[6]) By July, Behrens was sounding people out about the possibility of selling his house. By the end of the year, he was having discussions about becoming director of the Kunstgewerbeschule (School of Arts and Crafts) in Düsseldorf.

This school, which had been strongly criticized by, among others, Wilhelm Schäfer in 1902,[7] came partly under the aegis of the Prussian Ministry of Trade and Commerce in Berlin. Behrens' appointment owed much to the influence of the architect and civil servant Hermann Muthesius, who was returning at this point to Germany, from his celebrated position as cultural attaché to the German Embassy in London. In his new capacity at the Ministry of Trade, Muthesius applied lessons learned in England to promote reform of the schools of art and design, and he secured the appointment of a number of first class designers in key positions in those within his sphere of influence. Düsseldorf was one of the first of such establishments to be subject to drastic reformation.

Behrens wrote a long, enthusiastic and rather inconsequential letter to Muthesius in January 1903, about his new appointment.[8] He expressed his sense of excitement at having a new post that would enable him to 'directly serve the interests of the State', and to help to develop that 'national culture' which was, he said, an objective yearned for by so many of the leading figures of his generation in Germany. On the other hand, he wrote of reservations he had had about the Düsseldorf authorities and their 'conditions', and of his awareness that he would have to face opposition from many of the residual established staff of the school. Although he did not divulge any of his detailed plans—so many thoughts were 'whizzing about' in his head—he made it clear that priority would be given to what he called 'der fortschreitenden produktiven Kunst': the practical application of art to real problems, without which, he wrote, 'grey theory' would maintain its 'dreary domination'. He also expressed the hope that in his personal activity he would have the opportunity to engage in 'greater tectonic undertakings' than those offered within the framework of applied art alone; he did not see his whole satisfaction in the future coming from the concentration of his creative powers solely on applied art. Here we have a hint of his future activity with the AEG. Towards the end of the letter, Behrens wrote of the schools he intended to visit in the near future, in order to learn at first hand how progressive ideas might be put into practice. Vienna, he considered, was essential. He also planned to visit the Hague, London and, eventually, Glasgow.

He moved to Düsseldorf in March, and in the event made his journey to England in June. He wrote to Muthesius (24 June) shortly after his return. After first announcing the enlargement of his family with the birth of their third child (Heinz Viktor), he expressed his gratitude to Muthesius for having acted as his guide to England and Scotland. The last Sunday in England had been a beautiful day for him. He was especially grateful for his introduction to 'Miss Jekyll and Sir Chance' at their houses:

I cannot ever remember having seen so harmonious a union of glorious country, masterly art and human amiability than at Munstead Wood and Orchards. The English visit was a powerful stimulus to me in many respects. I still feel more and more what a deep impression that 'land of culture' made on me; certainly the strongest I have ever had from a country.

In another letter to Muthesius (9 August) he returned to the subject of his visit again:

I feel that I am sincerely indebted to you, now and for ever, for all the interesting things I saw and experienced in England and Scotland. As I have already said to you, this journey has brought me to really consolidate and confirm my conception of a modern culture, one that will be of lasting value to me, for the rest of my life.[9]

This note reminds one again of the intensity of Behrens' concern with the development of German culture. In the future, however, British influences on Behrens were relatively slight, despite the marvellous effect that those houses of Lutyens must have had on that summer day in the first maturity of their wonderful gardens.

In 1903, Behrens was able to appoint Rudolf Bosselt, the young sculptor from the Darmstadt colony, Fritz Ehmcke, the graphic designer from Berlin, and two young men from Vienna: the interior designer Max Benirschke and the painter Josef Bruckmüller. Behrens himself took charge of the architecture class. In the late summer, he approached Wassily Kandinsky, who was living at that time in Schwabing and who was a member of the *Vereinigung für angewandte Kunst* (Union for Applied Art), an organization which had grown out of the *Vereinigte Werkstätten* (of which Behrens had been a founder member in his Munich days). Kandinsky had been very active with woodcuts, a favourite medium of Behrens, and had also been designing handbags, tobacco-pouches, Ex-Libris labels and so on. This invitation, which anticipated Kandinsky's call to the Bauhaus by nearly twenty years, had to be refused as Kandinsky was on the point of leaving Germany for a period of extensive travel over a period of several years.[10]

One of the most interesting aspects of the Düsseldorf *Kunstgewerbeschule* was the setting up of preparatory courses. Behrens felt that it was essential for students to experience different aspects of artistic activity, and to learn techniques of observation and analysis before going on to specialize in a particular branch of design.[11]

The two *Vorbereitungsklassen* were taught by Benirschke and Bruckmül-ler, and were developed from their experience of the *Kunstgewerbeschule* in Vienna. Students on these courses made drawings and paintings of natural forms in different media; for example a spray of Honesty would be succes-sively drawn in charcoal, painted in colour, enlarged or analysed in detail and so on. A distinction was made between *Erscheinungszeichnen* (represen-tational drawings) and *Konturzeichnen* (outline drawings). These last draw-ings would make the analysis in pure line. Geometrical analyses and exer-cises were also made, and students were encouraged to make patterns from them; some were carried out with cut paper shapes, and some composi-tional studies based on such work were made in three dimensions, in wood, plaster or other materials. These innovatory courses were among the pre-cursors of the *Vorkurse* or Preliminary Courses of the Bauhaus and their descendants, familiar to us today as central features of the curricula of most schools of art. Behrens said in an interview a few years later:

Today's school of applied art has to meet both the demands of the handicrafts for aesthetic directives and the needs of industry for artistic impulses. The Düsseldorf School seeks a mediation by going back to the fundamental intellectual principles of all form-creating work, and allows the principles of form making to be rooted in the artistically spontaneous, in the inner laws of perception, rather than directly in the mechanical aspects of the work.

He was alert to developments in contemporary Dutch architecture, as he had been to Dutch painting during the 1890s. He wrote a number of letters to H. P. Berlage, whose celebrated *Beurs* in Amsterdam had just been com-pleted, inviting him to come to Düsseldorf. In the end, Berlage declined, but J. L. M. Lauweriks was put foward, and he joined Behrens' staff in 1904.[12]

Lauweriks was to have a modest but distinct influence on Behrens himself, on the School, its students and through them on German and Dutch architecture in general. Of his pupils at Düsseldorf, Adolf Meyer was to work with Behrens on the AEG factories, and later to become Gropius's retiring but underestimated partner.[13] Another, Fritz Kaldenbach, was a brilliant assistant to Gropius from 1914 until his death in 1918.

Lauweriks' particular contribution at Düsseldorf was the teaching of his own method of design based on a geometrical grid. This grid was basically evolved from a square, within which a circle was inscribed. From this simple figure, the grid was developed by subdividing and duplicating squares, and used as the definitive pattern for fixing the proportions and relative dimensions of every feature of a building, a piece of furniture, metal work, graphic design, typography or any other problem.

There was certainly a remarkable transformation in Behrens' style in 1904. All his outstanding projects of 1904 are in a new, severely geometrical style, with all the forms determined by squares, circles and triangles. The tendency he had undoubtedly had towards the use of simple geometrical forms, as seen earlier in the basic cube and pyramid of his Darmstadt house, or the Wertheim dining room, was from now on given much clearer expression.

A striking demonstration of architectural geometry was his garden layout and pavilion for the Düsseldorf *Gartenbau-und Kunstausstellung* of 1904. The axis of the garden—60 metres (196 ft) long and 30 metres (98 ft) wide-—was centred on the restaurant *Jungbrunnen* (Fountain of Youth) that served non-alcoholic refreshments. At this time Behrens was active in the temperance movement. Karl Scheffler explained the reason:

In his youth he became a close friend of the poet Hartleben. Many a night they sat drinking together. But his heart wasn't really in such extravagances. There came a crisis and a thorough cure. Overnight the young artist became very abstemious, drank nothing but water, and always had faith in one or other of those sort of doctors, who don't amount to much with their colleagues, but who know how to captivate their patients.[14]

Although the door of this restaurant was centred on the long axis of the garden, the building itself was slightly asymmetrical. Of the two slightly projecting wings on either side of the entrance, one was square in plan, the other rectangular. The rectangular wing and the central bay of the building had a flat roof-garden with a pergola on top that gave a horizontal roof-line to the greater part of the building. The left-hand wing (a little like a tall Georgian house) had a very shallow, low-pitched pyramidal roof behind a parapet of the same height as that of the pergola. The white, smooth beams, with dark, textured infilling panels of this little concrete building created the impression of an abstract architecture of spaces and shapes defined by white laths or sticks. (A nickname for Behrens was coined—'*Latzenpitter*'[15] ('Lattice-Peter') which neatly fuses an echo of the well-known '*Struwelpeter*' with laths and '*Latz*'—a bib—a derogatory reference to the non-alcoholic beverages he favoured). In harmony with the restaurant were rectangular pergolas of white lattice work, with a marble fountain on the cross axis halfway down the site. There was another smaller fountain, with a white marble statue of a youth by Bosselt. Marble benches executed in Bosselt's sculpture class at the *Kunstgewerbeschule* were also used in the garden, evidence of the policy of engaging students on projects for actual use.

The restaurant interior had walls hung with panels of printed cretonne stretched between white laths, and white furniture comprising little oval tables and Mackintosh-like ladder-backed chairs. Max Osborn remarked on

Düsseldorf Exhibition: Interior, Restaurant Jungbrunnen, 1904.

the Renaissance character of the garden, and explained that Behrens wished to design the garden as an extension of the interior of a house, imposing the decorative principles of his interiors on Nature outside: 'Habitable nature, a living room in the open air'.[16] Echoes of this approach can perhaps be seen in Le Corbusier's work in the 1920s.

The Düsseldorf exhibition was reviewed without much enthusiasm by Hans Singer in the *Studio*:

His attempt is a set design, and its distinct architectural aspect is the result of a deliberate intention. This explains what he aims at in framing his garden with woodwork, in assigning an important part to his electric lamp posts, in introducing a large fountain and basin on a low level in so relatively small a garden, and in laying out comparatively many and broad walks. There are hardly any flowers. The chief element in the design is the contrast presented by the pure white marble and painted woodwork, with the green grass and foliage.[17]

Behrens and Karl Ernst Osthaus

An important development for Behrens during 1904 was his growing friendship with Karl Ernst Osthaus. From him came Behrens' first two commissions for work in Hagen, Westphalia.

Karl Ernst Osthaus was a young patron of the arts, collector and scholar. The son of a banker, he had inherited a fortune from his maternal grandfather and decided to use his money to establish a museum in Hagen. In 1898, he had commissioned the Berlin architect Carl Gérard (architect of his father's house) to design a museum building, but when the shell of this rather dull Neo-Renaissance building was ready in 1900, Osthaus invited Henry van de Velde to come to Hagen and to design the interiors, the furniture and fittings. This Van de Velde did, clothing the existing steel structure of the interior with a light, elegant arcaded ensemble in the Art Nouveau style. It is believed that Van de Velde was also responsible for influencing Osthaus over the whole purpose of the museum. Be that as it may, when the Folkwang museum opened in July 1902, it was principally as a gallery of modern art. It was named after the palace of the goddess of beauty, Freia, in the *Nibelungensage*. In it, Osthaus formed the first great collection of contemporary European art to be open to the public on a regular basis, and the museum was also host to a series of important exhibitions, conferences and lectures.

Osthaus commissioned Behrens to design a lecture theatre for the museum and also brought him a commission to design an additional room for the house of a relation, the industrialist Alfred Harkort.

Behrens began the designs for the lecture theatre and the sitting room in January 1904. He sent Osthaus the final drawings for the lecture theatre as a Christmas present the following December. The lecture theatre was his first frankly Neo-Classical interior. It was designed for a semi-circular bay on the second floor of the existing fabric. Osthaus described it as follows:

The form of the lecture room can be described in remarkably few words. Against two juxtaposed cubes, a half-cylinder is set: a hemispherical dome of the same diameter completes the shape. As we only comprehend this form through the planes which bound it, so the inner life of the room can be realized as the product of its walls. In

Vortragsaal (Lecture Theatre) Folkwang Museum, Hagen, 1905. (Destroyed).

their relationship, however, lies the character of Behrens' decorative scheme. As the lines divide the wall into planes, so they also divide the room into layers. We see in their precipitation a rhythmical life, interchanging combinations derived from the use of a basic unit. This unit is a 75cm (29½in) square. It goes seven times into the height and the width of the square side walls. The vertical wall panels are from one to three units wide, and six high. Over them a horizontal frieze extends, of which the metopes and twin console brackets emphatically occupy one-unit squares. Doors, the cupboard and stove are of twelve units. So the room is filled with airy cubic spaces which interplay in every form, every line . . .[18]

There were two doors into the room, on the long rectangular wall, and some fixed seating on the semi-circular wall facing it. The only furniture was a lectern and the cupboards and heating unit mentioned by Osthaus. The dome was painted with square coffering. The contrast between this Neo-Classical room (destroyed by bombing in the Second World War) and the Van de Velde interiors of the Folkwang museum was very striking. It reflected Behrens' growing enthusiasm for classical art and architecture in a dramatic way. (Since his first visit to Italy with Hartleben, he had returned as often as possible. In the summer of 1904 he had spent most of his time in Pompeii and Rome, studying the antiquities.)

The other work of this period at Hagen was the sitting room for Harkort's house, the *Haus* Schede bei Wetter (Wetter is on the Ruhr near Hagen). It was completed early in 1905. It is an unusual feature, a large circular oriel built out from the corner of a fine early nineteenth-century house, and from which an attractive view over the garden and a wooded hillside can be seen. The room is virtually without walls, having large windows from floor to ceiling around most of its diameter. There is a small balcony round the outside. For this attractive room, Behrens also designed the furniture, fittings and carpet. The circular table and chairs echo the form of the room itself, whilst there are square motifs (like the blue carpet, reflected by a recess in the ceiling) in counter-point to the circles, which delineate the plan of the corner of the house. The woodwork was silver grey, the material covering the furniture blue, and the curtains were yellow. The room still exists in excellent condition.

The North West German Art Exhibition, 1905
An impressive interior, destroyed during the Second World War, was a reading room for the Düsseldorf City Library. It was exhibited, before its permanent installation in the *Kunstgewerbemuseum*, at the St Louis World's Fair of 1904. Behrens also designed the official catalogue of the German Imperial exhibition at the St Louis Fair. The library appears to have been severely rectangular in all its forms. It incorporated much decorative sculpture by Bosselt. A very striking feature when lit, apparently, were the cubic electric reading lamps and the row of white cubic lights overhead. The top surfaces of the reading desks were covered with white leather. Hoeber described the effect as 'Abstract mathematic brilliance'.

Other interior designs of this busy year were for Dr Mannhardt in Hamburg, and for the offices of Klöpper in the same city. He exhibited a dining-room in Dresden, and designed material for the *Hagener Textilindustrie*—printed cottons that were exhibited at St Louis.

The outstanding architectural works of 1905 were, however, an exhibition and a private house. For the *Nordwestdeutsche Kunstausstellung* (North-West German Art Exhibition) at Oldenburg, Behrens developed his Neo-Classical style even more radically than at Hagen. The exhibition took place in the summer, and for it Behrens designed a large, unified complex of buildings around a broad, rectangular open space. In the centre of this space was an octagonal orchestra pavilion with a cupola. Around its perimeter was a chain of long low white benches with little conifer bushes between them. At one end of the place was the main group of buildings: an exhibition hall in the form of a large near-cube with a pyramidal roof. Attached to each of its corners were smaller, flat-roofed cubes, and from these short colonnades led to two small cubic administrative pavilions that echoed the central hall in having pyramidal roofs. At the far end of the open space were two small free standing pavilions for commercial firms—on one side, that of the Rogge *Zigarrenfabrik* and on the other, that of the *Delmenhorster Linoleumfabrik*. This marked the beginning of an association with this firm that anticipated

North West German Art Exhibition, Oldenburg, 1905.

*North West German Art Exhibition: Rogge Zigarrenfabrik pavilion (left);
Delmenhorster Linoleumfabrik pavilion (right).*

Behrens' appointment with the AEG, albeit on a smaller scale. He designed
linoleum patterns, as well as their exhibition stands and their publicity
material.

The garden was flanked by white wooden pergolas and lattice pavilions
and niches repeating the same theme of cubes and hemispherical domes as
that of the main buildings.

In his 1913 book on Behrens, Fritz Hoeber demonstrated how the elevations of these buildings were designed with a schema based on rectangles
developed from isosceles triangles of 40°. He shows the relative proportion
of the central pavilion to the façades of the minor, flanking ones to be in a
ratio of 3:2 in area, and that all the major divisions and openings of the
façades lie on the lines of a grid. The designs on the surfaces of the buildings
make this underlying geometry obvious even to the casual eye—the smaller
cubic pavilions of the main group have, for example, a pattern decoration of
four vertical panels and a sort of frieze of 40° triangles and diamond shapes.

These stark white cubic buildings with their bold geometric surface patterns were novel in their form of Neo-Classicism, and in their suppression of material or constructional elements. They were of a pure geometry of planes set in pure relationships in space. Julius Meier-Graefe wrote an article on Behrens at this time, in which he asked:

Wouldn't it be possible to build in such a way that nothing of the form, but only the admirable cool spirit of the Greeks could once more be resurrected? There is no one form that could be borrowed. True Hellenism exists more clearly as an ideal than in the reality of the ruins . . .[19]

This no doubt echoes Behrens himself. He was perhaps trying to create a classicism without capitals, without carving or apparent construction, an apparently weightless architecture of pure form and space—a striking anticipation of the work of Mies van der Rohe in the 1920s.

Hoeber and others have called attention to the similarity between Behrens' geometrical grid and those used by the Dutch: Lauweriks, De Bazel and Berlage.[20] None of these contemporaries, well known to Behrens, were using such a method to create buildings that looked anything like Behrens' Neo-Classical compositions. However, Behrens was developing a highly individual, archaizing architectural style that was largely the fruit of his enthusiasm for Italy. Meier-Graefe wrote:

The way to the antique lies within our reach. But we must not stop at Greece, rather we must bring Hellenic clarity, Hellenic reason—or rather we might simply say beauty—into our forms. That is what Behrens is seeking.

In the context of the Oldenburg exhibition, and subsequent works by Behrens, the words 'Greece' and 'the Antique' may be taken to mean a curious fusion of ideas regarding archaic simplicity and purity of form. He had acquired them, not so much from Greek art itself, as from his observation of Romanesque architecture in Tuscany (the Baptistry of the Cathedral at Florence, for example, is a crystalline geometric form clothed in flat white sheets of material inlaid with bold abstract patterns) and from his study of the history and archaeology of classical art in general. Burckhardt, Riegl, Wölfflin, Wiegand and others were sources of inspiration, especially where they called attention to hitherto little-known or underestimated periods in antiquity—archaic Greek art, or late Roman, for example. Something of the way in which Behrens and his friends saw affinities between the arts of very different periods can be seen in a letter Dehmel wrote to Behrens in 1904:

Yes, the truly archaic antique (that is, up to 500 BC) can really bring us another creative blossoming, as has the elegance of the Attic. Such things as the lyre-playing Apollo and the two deer in Naples, as well as the Etruscan She-Wolf in Rome, have their exact equals only in early Romanesque architecture, and have unquestionable emotional power and stylistic drive, that is related to our own . . .[21]

The Obenauer House

The second private house to be designed by Behrens was for the industrialist Gustav Obenauer, at St Johann-Saarbrücken. The plans reached their final form in May 1905, and the house was begun in late 1905 and finished early in 1906. Although Behrens characteristically used a cube as the basis for the body of the house, and again gave it a pyramidal roof, the Obenauer house has an informal and organic composition, as it was built on a steeply sloping site, which affected the design of the house a good deal. The extensions to that basic cube, which was about 12 metres (38ft) square, such as the flat-roofed kitchen wing on the north-east (uphill) corner, and the terrace and pergola around the south and west sides of the house, tend to conceal the simple form at the heart of the design. The three-storey façade presented to Trillerweg is enlivened by the advancement and recession of various elements of the three almost equal horizontal levels: the entrance, with its terrace above, projects well in front of the two upper storeys; the top storey is jettied out slightly over the middle one. The centre bay of the upper storey recedes, however, but has a little curved balcony cantilevered out over the terrace below. Above the centre bay the façade is crowned with a small triangular pediment-like dormer in the (fourth) attic storey in the roof. The west side of the house is not dissimilar.

A Neo-Classical touch is given by the row of closely spaced, chunky

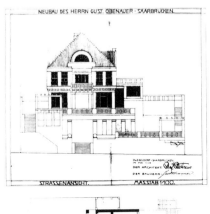

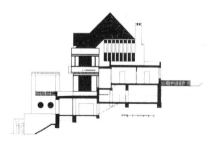

Obenauer House, Saarbrücken, 1905: Elevation (above left); Cross-section (above right); Plan (left).

63

Obenauer House, Saarbrücken, 1905.

dentils under the slight projection of the upper storey, a motif repeated as a lintel over the main entrance, which is flanked by short cylindrical columns on either side. The east and north-east sides of the house have a number of details reminiscent of Voysey or Mackintosh: groups of mullioned windows, and tall chimneys with flat tops. The motifs of a circle within a square, and variations on subdivided squares appear in the ironwork and on the plaster ceilings as well as the furnishings of the house. Behrens designed a study-library in the house a few years later, in 1910.

The Concert Hall in Cologne and the Crematorium at Hagen

In 1905 Behrens showed a bedroom and a living room in another exhibition of modern interiors at Wertheim's store in Berlin; he also designed the installation of the *Deutsche Jahrhundertausstellung* (an exhibition of paintings) at the National Gallery in Berlin, and produced a memorable poster for the exhibition.

He was, furthermore, engaged in the design of a number of projects which were to be realized during the following year. The most important of these were for exhibitions: the third *Deutsche Kunstgewerbeausstellung* in Dresden, and the *Tonhaus* (concert hall) for the art exhibition in the Flora Garden in Cologne. Both these schemes were used by Behrens as a field for experiment in an architecture of pure geometry in the spirit of early Christian and Tuscan Romanesque religious buildings.

By this time, moreover, Behrens was having much correspondence with Osthaus over commissions that the Maecenas of Hagen was arranging for him: the principal of these was for a crematorium at Delstern. The crematorium, the first in Prussia, was the enterprise of the *Verein für Feuerbestattung* of Hagen, and Osthaus had been approached for artistic advice about its design. The chairman of the *Verein*, a member of the Board of Health, Dr Müller, sent Osthaus a macabre sketch, prepared by a *Baumeister* Sanders, for a Gothic revival folly, incorporating a castellated tower and an attendant's lodge. The tower could be connected to the crematorium by an underground passage, suggested Dr Müller, so that the smoke could be drawn through a chimney inside it, affording the practical advantage of providing central heating for the little house. This bizarre idea was not taken any further by Behrens and Osthaus, who undertook to provide the plans for a crematorium free of charge.

A long letter from Behrens of May 1905 to Osthaus discussed many aspects of his ideas and plans for it.[22] (That letter is, incidentally, typewritten. Earlier letters to Osthaus are all handwritten by a clerk or more rarely by Behrens himself). Behrens eventually had the idea of making the concert hall for the Cologne exhibition into a trial study for the crematorium; a curious idea at first sight, but one which offered the opportunity to make a large-scale mock-up of the proposed building (which was, in its essentials, no more than a hall) and to make it possible to offer the *Verein* a set of plans, the cost of which had already been covered.[23]

Concert Hall in the Flora Garden, Cologne, 1906: Entrance.

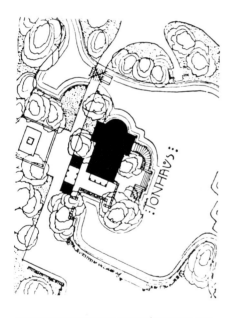

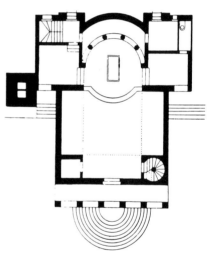

(Above left) Concert Hall in the Flora Garden: Plan.

(Above right) Crematorium, Delstern, 1906–7: Plan.

(Left) Crematorium: Organ case.

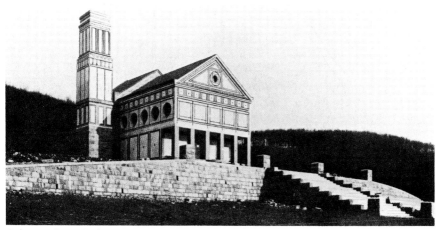

Crematorium, Delstern, 1906–7.

The basic form resembled a small early Christian or Romanesque church with galleries. It was, however, without nave arcading under the galleries, and thus had no distinction between nave and side aisles. There was (and is, in the case of the crematorium, which still stands) a narthex across the entrance, with an organ loft above. The organ case is decorated with a pattern resembling those in the giant scrolls on the façade of Santa Maria Novella in Florence. At the other end a semi-circular domed apse with columns terminates the hall, beyond shallow transepts. In the concert hall, the crossing between the nave and transepts was clearly defined between two big semi-circular arches (triumphal arches in early Christian terms), both decorated in the spandrels with octagonal spiral patterns. The space between them over the sanctuary was glazed, the flat ceiling having glazing bars in a pattern of circles within squares. From this ceiling hung a circle of lights. The dome of the apse was decorated with a mosaic by E. R. Weiss in the style of those at Ravenna, although without specific Christian icono-graphy. Three youths kneel on the flower-studded grass, between trees, against a gold background. The centre figure raises his hands with the gesture of St Apollinaris in the mosaic in the basilica at Classe; above are the words *'Alles vergängliche ist nur ein Gleichnis'* ('All that perishes is but a parable').

The body of the hall was lit, as was the later crematorium, by five large round windows above the galleries on each side. The concert hall was built on a romantic site, on a promontory on a little ornamental lake. Half hidden by trees, it could only be reached through an attached propylaeum, or across the lake, to where a flight of steps came down to the water's edge. Behrens designed the piano for the hall. He expressed the hope that the music played there would accord with what he called the *Gesamtkünstlichen* (artistically unified) design of the building as a whole. He resurrected his plans to stage

Dehmel's '*Eine Lebensmesse*' again, and again without success. The exhibition opened in May 1906, and Behrens' *Tonhaus* contrasted sharply with the nearby *Frauen Rosenhof* pavilion by Olbrich, which was essentially an Art Nouveau work.

As for the crematorium itself, it closely followed the design of the *Tonhaus*. The mosaic by E. R. Weiss was recreated in the apse. The sanctuary was somewhat simplified, and one of the triumphal arches was omitted. There were changes in the ground plan, necessitated by the provision of a vestry and waiting room for the next-of-kin, and a room for the coffin on one side of the sanctuary. The catafalque was designed to sink into the basement at the height of the service. A tall rectangular chimney, resembling a campanile, was attached to the building.

The whole aspect of the crematorium is strongly reminiscent of San Miniato al Monte above Florence, and its position, on a steeply sloping hillside, is very similar. Behrens' building, clad in marble, proved to be very expensive. It was finished in June 1907, but there was recurrent trouble over the years as the marble sheeting came loose. Today the exterior is very much altered, having a dull, rendered finish. The long, low columbarium behind the crematorium was never built.[24]

The Dresden Exhibition, 1906

The other major task of 1905–6 was the design of exhibition buildings for the third *Deutsche Kunstgewerbeausstellung* (Exhibition of Applied Art) in Dresden. This exhibition, like that in Cologne, took place during the summer of 1906. Behrens was a regional director, and was responsible for the exhibition rooms of the *Düsseldorfer Kunstgewerbeschule*, his own school, and for an independent group of buildings comprising a concert hall opening on to a small, enclosed courtyard, a vestibule and a reception room.[25] He also designed a pavilion for the *Delmenhorster Linoleumfabrik*.

The concert hall was rectangular with side aisles, its semi-circular barrel vaulted nave being supported on four rectangular pillars. This interior, like those of the buildings described earlier, was white, with bold patterns drawn from a variety of antique and Italian Romanesque sources, and with a frieze of squares above the pillars emphasizing the geometry of the design. The square atrium-like courtyard opened directly from this room, and had a cloister on three sides: thick cylindrical columns resting on a low wall. These supported a blind arcade. The sunken centre of the courtyard, wholly tiled, had as its sole feature a life-sized statue of a youth by Rudolf Bosselt, placed on a square tiled plinth in the centre. This ensemble can be seen as the third variant of the themes explored in the Hagen and Cologne buildings.

The *Delmenhorster* pavilion, for the *Ankermarke* (Anchor Brand) linoleum works, was a novel venture; a little octagonal building with a hemispherical dome on a cylindrical drum. It was set, like the *Tonhaus*, by water. Four of the facets of the octagon were extended to make a cruciform plan, one arm of which was the porch, supported on near-Doric columns, complete with entasis. The interior, like the exterior, was white, with bands of black decoration. Inside there were little octagonal pillars.

Behrens used the image of this little *tempietto* for the cover of the firm's prospectus, and further developed his range of patterns for their products. It is possible that this exhibition pavilion, the products and the brochure were responsible for drawing the attention of Paul Jordan, the AEG director, to Behrens and his work. He may have read the article by Ernst Schur in *Die Rheinlande* (a review of the Dresden exhibition) in which he hailed Behrens

(Above) Third German Exhibition of Applied Art, Dresden, 1906: Delmenhorster Linoleumfabrik Pavilion.

(Left) Third German Exhibition of Applied Art: Exterior of the Concert Hall (with Bosselt sculpture removed).

69

Tapetenhaus Klein, Hagen, 1905–7: Entrance (Destroyed).

as an artist peculiarly gifted for and suited to working with industry: 'Behrens has, at the moment, a position in Germany that is indisputable—he works with industry and puts fresh life into it'.[26]

Further projects at Hagen

Osthaus was responsible for involving Behrens in several further commissions in Hagen during the period 1905/6. Plans for one of these, a shop for the firm of *Josef Klein*, were completed in December 1905, and the shop fitted out during 1906–7. On one side of its square plan, a deep entry led right through to the stairs, while the door to the shop itself was on one side. The entry, like the interior of the shop, had a coffered ceiling with an electric light in the centre of each coffer, similar in design to the dining-room ceiling of the Obenauer house. The staircase door had an amusing pediment of Neo-Classical spirals, of the same pattern as those published with his typographical ornaments for his Kursiv type. The *Tapetenhaus Klein*, which sold wallpapers and fabrics, was destroyed during the Second World War, although the firm still exists in Hagen.

A design for a *Milchhäuschen* (a kiosk for the sale of milk) was eventually rejected by the milk marketing organization of Hagen (December 1905). A very much larger and more important project, for a new Protestant church to be built in Hagen-Wehringhausen, finally came to nothing in 1907, even though Behrens worked on plans for it throughout 1906. The Evangelical Church Community of Hagen, led by Pastor Kayser, also considered designs by another architect, Fritz Schumacher. Behrens made two principal designs, one with a nave, a Latin cross in plan, the other octagonal. Behrens favoured the octagonal church, and in his submission stressed that he had considered the way in which the church, the pastor's house and the ancillary buildings would fit into the urban environment. He also touched on the Carolingian derivation of its style:

The architecture of this project is bound up with the tradition of the Carolingian period, (especially notable in the western part of Germany), although, whilst therein recognizing the main artistic guidelines, suffering no detriment to the creation of an entirely modern form as demanded by the contemporary Protestant cult.[27]

The church authorities did not, however, like it.

Design for a Protestant church, Hagen, 1906–7.

71

Design for the Tietz department store, Düsseldorf, 1906.

They made a great to-do with rules and compasses, they found the windows too small and the towers not pointed enough, made comparisons with factories and cowsheds, and found hardly any redeeming quality in either Schumacher or Behrens.

So wrote Osthaus, who published one or two articles, both locally and nationally, bitterly attacking the outcome. He had done his best to involve imaginative architects in the project.

When someone has plans by Behrens and Schumacher in hand, and then calls in Siebold and Plange, one can only bury one's head in one's hands.[28]

The architect Plange from Elberfeld was eventually given preference.

Perhaps the most interesting outcome of this abortive project was the use Behrens made of his rejected plans for the octagonal church, when he designed his first work for the AEG—the pavilion for the German Ship-building Exhibition in Berlin in 1908.

An interesting competition design, also prepared late in 1906, was for the store *Warenhaus Leonhard Tietz* to be built in the Königsallee, Düsseldorf. (Olbrich in fact won the competition). This also looks forward to the work Behrens was to do for the AEG: the side façade of the *Warenhaus Tietz*, with its impressive stepped rows of windows descending from the staircase towers at either end, is distinctly like the façade of the great *Hochspannungs-fabrik* of 1910.

About this time, Behrens sent Osthaus the first of the site plans for the Eppenhausen *Gartenvorstadt* (Garden Suburb) that his patron was to create around his new house near Hagen. This will be discussed later.

The Mannheim Exhibition, 1906–7

Before the end of the year, Behrens began to make his first designs for the AEG. These were modest enough, and confined to graphic design. He made the layout and lettering design of the binding for Volume II (the year's numbers for 1906) of the *Mitteilungen der Berliner Electricitäts-Werke* (Bulletin of the BEW, a subsidiary of the AEG).[29]

A major task towards the end of 1906 was, however, the design of a room for the International Art Exhibition due to take place in Mannheim in May 1907. Behrens' room was in the new *Kunsthalle*, the architect of which was Hermann Billing. Behrens went to some trouble to choose the exhibits for this room, so that they would make a harmonious ensemble. The focus of the arrangement was a cast of Maillol's *'Méditerranée'*, set before a niche in the end wall. (The original belonged to Harry Graf Kessler, Maillol's German friend and patron. Kessler encouraged Osthaus to buy Maillol's *'La Nymphe'* about this time.) Other works by Maillol, Bourdelle and Bernhard Hoetger were in the room, along with paintings by Hermann Haller and Christian Rohlfs, one of Osthaus's favourite artists, and who had been induced by him to live in Hagen.

Exhibition Hall, International Art Exhibition, Mannheim, 1907: Interior.

The works of art were displayed against a background of plain walls. Above the height of the doors, the wall and ceiling surfaces were divided into plain rectangular panels. Decoration was restricted to the square recessions in the ceiling, to a narrow band above the plain walls, and to a minimal triangular pediment above each door.

Heinrich Wölfflin, the great Swiss art historian, visited the exhibition with a companion, Fritz Wichert, in the autumn of 1907, when they were staying nearby in Darmstadt for the International Congress on the History of Art. They were agreed that Behrens' room was the best in the exhibition, and Wölfflin is reported to have expressed the opinion that Behrens would 'surely have a great future as an architectonic artist if he could unite his eurhythmy of line and plane with a cubic beauty like that which makes the Palazzo Strozzi in Florence a classic building'. Hoeber, who quoted this observation (in his 1913 book on Behrens) felt that it was prophetic of Behrens' achievement in Berlin.[30]

Behrens was also responsible for a garden at Mannheim. It was not unlike his Düsseldorf and Oldenburg gardens, in that it was an arrangement of lattice arbours and pergolas around formal, axially planned spaces. There was also a little open air theatre.

When one considers that Behrens also had to prepare a special room of his work for the *Kunstausstellung* to take place in the summer of 1907, it is not surprising that he fell ill with overwork in the spring of that year, and had to spend about a month of convalescence at the Hotel Nizza in Wiesbaden.

Notes

1. The Nürnberg and Düsseldorf courses are discussed in detail in Stanford Anderson op. cit., p132, also n13, p170ff. See also Exhibition Catalogue, *Peter Behrens und Nürnberg*, Germanisches Nationalmuseum, Nürnberg, Prestel, 1980; Nikolaus Pevsner, *Academies of Art Past and Present*, New York, Da Capo Press, 1973, and Hans Wingler (Ed.), *Kunstschulreform 1900–1933*, Berlin, Gebr. Mann Studio-Reihe, 1977.
2. W. Fred, 'The International Exhibition of Modern Decorative Art at Turin: The German Section', *Studio*, vol XXVII, 1903, pp188–97.
3. L. Gmelin, *Die erste internationale Ausstellung für moderne dekorative Kunst in Turin 1902: Kunst und Handwerk*, November 1902, p293ff.
4. Fritz Hoeber, *Peter Behrens* op. cit., p221.
5. Max Osborn, *Die modernen Wohnräume im Warenhaus von A. Wertheim in Berlin: Deutsche Kunst und Dekoration*, Yr. IV, vol 6, March 1903, pp263, 291–3.
6. Dehmel, *Ausgewählte Briefe 1902–1920* op. cit.
7. W. Schäfer, 'Moderne Stil', *Die Rheinlande*, June 1902, pp48, 51–53.
8. A letter now in the Werkbund Archiv, Muthesius file. Reproduced in *Werkbund 3*, Berlin 1978.
9. Letters in the Muthesius file of the Werkbund Archiv, Berlin.
10. '. . . Yesterday Professor Peter Behrens came to me and asked me to take over

the direction of a class for decorative painting at the Düsseldorf Arts and Crafts School.'

From a letter to Gabriele Münter, 30 August 1903, quoted in Peg Weiss, 'Kandinsky and the Jugendstil Arts & Crafts Movement', Burlington Magazine, May 1975, pp290–75. Kandinsky included work by Behrens in the first Phalanx Society exhibition which he organized in Schwabing. He visited Behrens in Düsseldorf in the spring of 1904. Peg Weiss maintains that Behrens' ideas on theatre reform influenced those of Kandinsky. See Weiss, Kandinsky and the Munich Artist's Theatre, Princeton, 1973, Chapter IX.

11. Dr H. Board, 'Die Kunstgewerbeschule zu Düsseldorf', Dekorative Kunst, Yr. VII, vol II, August 1904, and in Kaiserslautern, Peter Behrens op. cit. p26.

12. See Pieter Singelenberg, H. P. Berlage, Idea and Style, Utrecht, Haentjens Dekker & Gumbert, 1972, p158.

13. One of Meyer's student drawings from Düsseldorf was used by Berlage as an illustration in his Grundlage und Entwicklung der Architektur, 1908, p56. Lauweriks, incidentally, described Meyer in a letter to De Bazel as 'one of my best pupils, considered the most familiar with working with systems'.

14. Karl Scheffler, Die fetten und die mageren Jahre op. cit.

15. Stanford Anderson op. cit., p179, n36.

16. Max Osborn, Die Düsseldorfer Ausstellung: Kunst und Künstler Yr. II, vol 12, Sept 1904, pp501–3.

17. Hans Singer, in 'Studio Talk', Studio, Vol XXXII, 1904, pp356–58.

18. Karl Ernst Osthaus, 'Peter Behrens', Kunst und Künstler IV, vol 3, 1907, p117.

19. Julius Meier-Graefe, 'Peter Behrens—Dusseldorf', Dekorative Kunst, VIII July 1905, pp381–428.

20. Berlage used the so-called 'Egyptian Triangle' described by Viollet-le-Duc, which has a relationship of height to base of 5:8. Behrens appears to have used a 40° isosceles triangle very close to this in shape, but giving broader, lower harmonies and intervals.

21. Dehmel, Ausgewählte Briefe 1902–1920 op. cit., No. 418, 5 October 1904.

22. Letter of 26 May 1905 now in the Karl Ernst Osthaus Archiv, Hagen, filed as Kü 410.

23. Letter now in KEO Archiv Kü 408, No. 17.

24. Behrens was not alone in this use of historicism: Gropius's model factory for the 1914 Werkbund exhibition in Cologne can be considered in Neo-Romanesque terms, as it is laid out like a basilican church with atrium.

25. The III deutsche Kunstgewerbeausstellung opened on 12 May 1906. Behrens was responsible for exhibits from the Rhineland. The exhibition is recognized as the source of inspiration for the formation of the Werkbund.

26. Die Rheinlande No. 12, 1906, p56ff. (A review of the Dresden exhibition.)

27. Karl Ernst Osthaus Archiv: Kü 416. Letter of 20 July 1907.

28. K. E. Osthaus, 'Eine Predigtkirche von Peter Behrens', Kunst und Künstler, Yr. IV, Vol 3, December 1907, pp121–4. There are recent discussions of this episode in Herta Hesse-Frielinghaus, Peter Behrens und Karl Ernst Osthaus, Dokumentation nach den Bestanden des Osthaus-Archivs, Hagen, 1966; Herta Hesse-Frielinghaus

(Ed.), *Karl Ernst Osthaus, Leben und Werk* op. cit., and Werner Gerber, *Nicht Gebaute Architektur; Peter Behrens und Fritz Schumacher als Kirchenplaner in Hagen, Beispiele aus den Jahren 1906–1907*, Hagen, Linnepe, 1980.

29. *The Berliner Electricitäts-Werke* was the Berlin Electrical Utility Corporation, developed by the AEG and reverting to the municipality in 1915. From No. 1 of Year III (January 1907), the report itself was designed by Behrens for several years.

30. Hoeber op. cit., p72. Wölfflin wrote in March 1908 to his parents that Peter Behrens was to give drawing courses to his art history students 'out of pure sympathy for my kind of Art History'.

6 Behrens and the AEG

His appointment

It is not known precisely how Behrens came to be employed by the AEG, nor who exactly was instrumental in negotiating his employment, nor what the terms of his contract really were.

It seems likely that Paul Jordan, *Baurat* in charge of the factories on the Humbolthain in Berlin, Director and one of the three most important men in the AEG, was immediately responsible. P. J. Cremers, in his 1928 book on Behrens, specifically names the Director Paul Jordan 'and not, as often written, Rathenau'[1] (that is, Emil Rathenau, the founder and Managing Director of the firm) as the person who called Behrens to Berlin as 'artistic advisor'. Behrens could, presumably, have easily corrected this statement at the time, had he disagreed. On the other hand, it is not understood how Behrens' work for the AEG rapidly expanded beyond the companies and activities of the corporation controlled by Jordan.

Behrens had, however, many friends in common with Walther Rathenau, the son of Emil. Walther Rathenau, a man of brilliant intellectual potential, a scientist and industrial magnate, also valued his friendships with artists and writers of distinction: Max Reinhardt, for example, Stefan Zweig, Hugo von Hofmannsthal, Rainer Maria Rilke, Henry van de Velde, Edvard Munch (who painted his portrait) and Franz Blei, who had written about Behrens in the *Studio* in 1901. Rathenau was a cousin of Max Liebermann, one of Behrens' earliest mentors, and he enjoyed mental gymnastics, like exchanging telegrams in verse with Richard Dehmel.

Although there is scant documentary evidence of the connection between Behrens and Walther Rathenau, a letter to the writer Maximilian Harden from Behrens has survived (of December 1905) in which he speaks at length of his enthusiasm for *'freund* Rathenau' and of their mutual friendship. Another of February 1906 invites Harden to dinner at the Hotel Bristol in Berlin along with Rathenau, as Behrens' guest.[2] By 1909, at any rate, Rathenau was writing to Behrens as *'Lieber Freund'* ('Dear Friend') and signing himself *'Herzlichst Ihr'* ('With all my heart, yours').[3]

Whatever the initial circumstances of his joining the firm, Behrens' reputation was obviously familiar to the most important people at the head of the AEG by 1907.

The *Allgemeine Elektricitäts-Gesellschaft* (General Electric Company) was (and is, as *AEG-Telefunken*) a vast industrial concern, originally built up by the engineer Emil Rathenau. Rathenau had acquired the German rights for the manufacture of Thomas Alva Edison's patented electric light system. He had seen Edison's incandescent light bulbs when they were first exhibited in Europe, at the Paris *Exposition Internationale de l'Électricité* in 1881, and two years later he formed the *Deutsche Edison Gesellschaft für angewandte Elektrizität*: the nucleus of the AEG. A few years later (1887) the company freed itself from licensing agreements, and changed its name to the AEG.

It was one of the most rapidly expanding companies at the turn of the century in Germany. By 1907 it had become one of the biggest manufacturers in the world of generators, cables, transformers, motors, light bulbs and arc lamps, quite apart from being responsible for the design and construction of power stations at home and abroad. (Walther Rathenau was in charge of the building of one in Manchester, England, for example). The AEG was, wrote Walther Rathenau in 1907, 'undoubtedly the largest European combination of industrial units under a centralized control and with a centralized organization'. In his 1928 biography of Rathenau, Harry Graf Kessler listed fifty-six companies, including mining, railways, aircraft manufacturers and rolling mills in this industrial empire. In the twenty-four years since its foundation, the concern had grown to employ 34,000 people in the main, parent factories alone.

Emil Rathenau pioneered all the fundamentals of modern large-scale industrial development. Starting with the mass production of cheap electric light bulbs, he brought together many sources of capital investment and, with his close associates Felix Deutsch, Paul Mamroth and Paul Jordan, developed a whole new province of industry. Their policy was one of expansion, until the company controlled every aspect of the means of production and distribution of electric light and power. This was extended to involve every branch of industry and locomotion in the country.

The AEG had already employed first-rate architects and designers. Franz Schwechten (the architect of the *Kaiser Wilhelm Gedächtniskirche* at the end of the Kurfürstendamm, now the lugubrious ruin preserved as a symbolic memorial to the Second World War) designed the principal buildings of the AEG factory on Ackerstrasse in 1894, and, in 1896, the amusing arched entrance to the *Maschinenfabrik* and other buildings on the Brunnenstrasse site in Berlin. Behrens' friend Otto Eckmann did many graphic and typographical designs for the AEG, and Alfred Messel (best known for the Wertheim store) designed the headquarters of the AEG on the Friedrich-Karl-Ufer (1905).

Behrens wrote a letter of thanks to Karl Ernst Osthaus,[4] on the eve of his departure from Düsseldorf, for his patronage, collaboration and friendship. For Behrens it was an exceptionally warmly expressed letter; throughout their long association—some seventeen years—most surviving letters are very formal and even distant in style. It is clear from the tone of this letter that the new job represented a dramatically new phase in his life, and that he was consciously marking the occasion with a sort of envoi. The following month, August 1907, Osthaus sent Behrens a watercolour by Rohlfs as a gift to mark the departure for Berlin.

The first public notice of Behrens' appointment was in the magazine *Werkkunst*,[5] where it was noted that the AEG 'had engaged Peter Behrens of Düsseldorf to design artistic shapes for arc lamps and all accessories'.[6]

Following a holiday in Italy, Behrens moved to an hotel in Berlin in October 1907, and undertook the modification of an old house he rented for himself and his family, the Erdmannshof house at Neubabelsberg, near Potsdam. In the garden he had a large studio constructed, and he began to build up a team to assist him in his new work. One of his earliest assistants in the Neubabelsberg atelier was Adolf Meyer, then aged twenty-six, who had been one of the outstanding pupils at Düsseldorf as a cabinet maker. Walter Gropius, then aged twenty-four, and a qualified architect, may have started with Behrens before the end of 1907, although the exact date is not known. (Gropius made contradictory statements about it. In *Apollo in der Demokratie*[7] he said that he began with Behrens in 1907, whilst in a letter to Frau Dr Herta Hesse-Frielinghaus shortly before his death, he wrote:

I was nearly a year in Spain during 1907–8, and there I met Osthaus for the first time; soon a close friendship grew up with him . . . Osthaus brought me to my Master, Peter Behrens . . .[8]

It is interesting to know of the rôle played in this by the ubiquitous Osthaus.)

Whilst the contract with the AEG may not have specified architectural advice or practice on Behrens' part, a notice in *Werkkunst* in September 1907[9] describes his work as involving the design of everything 'which in the widest sense of the word is connected with interior design'. It is clear that Behrens had every intention of further developing the architectural and interior design side of his work, and that he was free to undertake work outside the AEG contract.

Arc Lamps
Some years later, Behrens wrote:

My activity with the AEG began above all with the design of some arc lamps . . . in collaboration with Jordan, who was properly speaking my client and my friend.[10]

Hoeber dated the first designs for arc lamps from early 1907.[11] Arc lamps were hanging lamps intended for public buildings: factories, warehouses, railway stations and so on. Some were with metal reflectors giving indirect light, and some had white or frosted glass globes.

Apart from a few specialized uses, arc lamps are no longer commonly employed today, as filament lamps have been developed to surpass their performance in every way. They worked by passing an electric current across the gap between two carbon electrodes: the stream of electrons and ions between the anode and the cathode released energy in the form of heat and brilliant white light. They were, in 1907, among the latest developments in electric lighting, having first been evolved in the 1890s. They had considerable advantages over gas lamps: although the initial costs were higher for installation, their light was some 300 times brighter, and yet they cost less to run. Lamps could be hung anywhere, connected to light-weight flexible wires rather than to a rigid system of gas pipes. They were less of a fire risk in theatres or factories, as they burned relatively coolly, and they were better for the atmosphere in such places, as they used only a negligible amount of oxygen. Against this, there were some disadvantages. Open arc lamps burned away their carbon rods very quickly; a 10 ampère lamp required 25–50mm (1–2ins) of carbon rod per hour. Lamps had a range of 8–20 hours burning time before the carbon rods had to be replaced. They had, consequently, to be easy to take to pieces for this frequent attention.

The form of these lamps tended almost inevitably to have three major sections. The top contained the electrical connections, and the mechanism designed·to hold the two long carbon rods. This mechanism, contained in a domed cylindrical casing, kept the rods adjusted for length and gap as the carbon burned away by means of electro-magnets; clockwork had been used at first.

The second part was a long cylindrical section which concealed the rods, and the third basic element of the lamp casing, the reflector or diffuser, covered the point where the two rods converged, as the light was too bright to be used unshielded. The lamp was suspended on a pulley and lowered from the ceiling. The body of the lamp was fixed together with large clips, which could be undone with the help of a metal grip projecting at right angles to the lamp. The functional details were unavoidable features of the appearance of the lamps.

It can be seen that there was little room for improvement in redesigning these lamps, and many of Behrens' designs were simply better proportioned versions of earlier models manufactured by the AEG.[12] Many of the earlier models in production were plain, unselfconscious industrial designs. It is true that the AEG did market lamps with vaguely rococo applied surface decoration previous to Behrens' arrival (and even after it), but his designs were not such a revolutionary innovation in terms of a 'pure machine aesthetic' as has generally been supposed. His approach resolved

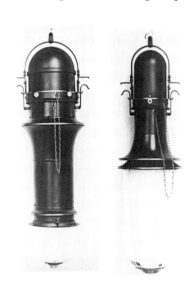

AEG Arc Lamps (Intensiv Flammenbogenlampen), 1908.

itself rather into one of making the mouldings and joints as few and as simple as possible; of designing curved profiles for the reflectors and glass diffusers; of consideration for the overall sculptural properties and the proportions. In this he proved to be brilliant.

For the proportions of the lamp as a whole, he may have had recourse to a grid system à la Lauweriks. Gropius also designed some of the appliances. He wrote to Helmut Weber in 1958:

I also occupied myself with the doctrine that Behrens had developed about 1906. For many a year I was constantly with Behrens in the evening at his house, and I identified myself with all his work, also with the many appliances for the AEG.[13]

Many of the lamps have shapes and profiles reminiscent of Greek kylixae and amphorae of which Behrens had a fine personal collection.[14] The colours—light or dark green lacquer, relieved by gold or bronze banding on the rims and mouldings—were discreet, smart and sober, well suited to the forms.

The Behrens lamps were enormously successful. According to Franz Mannheimer, the AEG invested 200,000 marks in the design and construction of prototypes and models for Behrens' arc lamps, and this was recovered in one year, due to production savings and increased sales.[15] Early in 1909, Wolf Dohrn (business manager of the Werkbund) reported that the AEG salesmen were very pleased with the new designs, and that they had said, perhaps a little naïvely, that they would welcome such a design approach to the interior, working parts.[16] The enterprise of Paul Jordan was handsomely rewarded; Behrens later quoted a shrewd observation of Jordan's that illustrates the basis of his thinking about industrial design:

AEG price list for electric kettles, 1913.

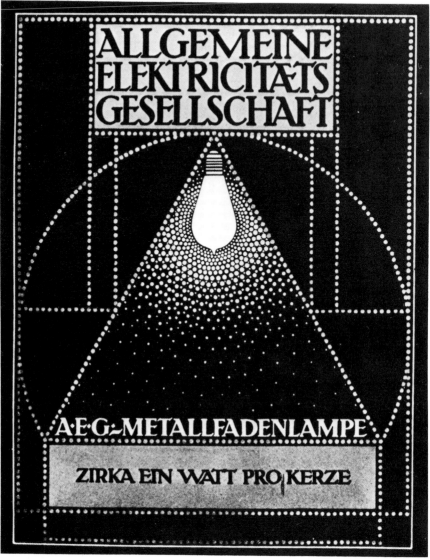

AEG Advertisement, 1907. Colour lithograph 67 × 52 cm (26¼ × 20¼ in).

Don't think that even an engineer, when he buys a motor, takes it to bits in order to scrutinize it. Even he as a specialist buys from the external appearance. A motor ought to look like a birthday present.[17]

Behrens designed many other electrical appliances for the AEG over the next few years: kettles, coffee pots, fans, clocks, dentist's drills and so on, all of a bold, simple and satisfying shape. His electric radiators, though, were rather strangely based on Carolingian reliquary-boxes.

Architecture for the AEG

The first buildings for the AEG by Behrens were, not surprisingly, exhibition pavilions and stands. In 1907, at the beginning of his appointment, he designed a little lattice construction along the lines of his Oldenburg garden pergolas for an industrial exhibition in June. It bore his new monogram for the AEG, a mildly Art Nouveau design of curved letters in a circle. A second work was the stand for the NAG (*Neue-Automobil-Gesellschaft*, a subsidiary of the AEG for the manufacture of cars and lorries) at the International Motor Show in Berlin in December.

More important was the AEG pavilion for the first German Shipbuilding Exhibition. This was a semi-permanent free-standing building that was open for four months, from June 1908 onwards. While the main exhibition took place in the official exhibition halls in the Zoological Gardens (Hardenbergstrasse), the AEG pavilion was built independently in the Auguste-Viktoria-Platz, and was conceived, according to Behrens, in relationship to the shape of the square. It also confronted the famous *Kaiser Wilhelm Gedächtniskirche* by Franz Schwechten (who had, as has been mentioned, worked for the AEG in 1889, 1896 and 1899). Behrens was probably conscious of challenging the Memorial church and its designer (the favourite architect of both Kaiser Wilhelm II and Emil Rathenau). His own building, although by no means free from historicism, with its bare, undecorated, smooth surfaces must have contrasted sharply with the eclectic Gothic revival church. The scorn felt by the younger generation for Schwechten's work is known from an anecdote concerning Walther Rathenau in 1912, when he described the *Gedächtniskirche* as typifying *kitsch*.

The *Schiffbauausstellung* pavilion was an octagonal building with a low-pitched roof, once more evolved from Tuscan Romanesque and earlier sources of inspiration. It is strongly reminiscent of a number of such buildings: the Baptistry of the Cathedral in Florence; Charlemagne's little Palatine Chapel at Aachen; San Vitale at Ravenna. It is, of course, also a simplification of his design for an octagonal church at Hagen. Gropius did the detailing of the pavilion.[18]

Two of the walls of the octagon, 18 metres (58 ft) in diameter and 20 metres (65 ft) high were extended, one into a high pedimented bay with five narrow windows, the other into a lower rectangular annexe with a pitched roof. The entrance, on the west front, faced the main exhibition halls. The remaining walls were decorated with a large blind arch between the two extensions containing three windows. The main light into the interior came from rows of windows all round the top third of the building, like a lantern. The exterior bore a new 'logo' or monogram for the AEG, with the letters disposed within a hexagon.

Inside, the pavilion displayed AEG products, especially, of course, those applicable to marine engineering. In the rectangular bay with the tall windows, a complete ship's bridge was installed. The interior was illuminated at night by an enormous octagonal pendant light fitting (a modern equivalent

AEG Pavilion, First German Shipbuilding Exhibition, Berlin, 1908.

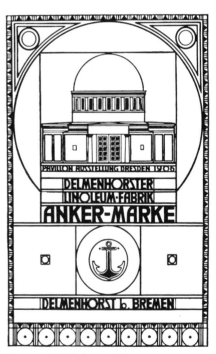

*Posters for the Delmenhorster Linoleumfabrik, 1906 (right), and the AEG
Pavilion, First German Shipbuilding Exhibition, 1908 (left).*

of the great octagonal corona of Friedrich I Barbarossa at Aachen) from which hung sixteen of Behrens' arc lamps.

Outside, at night, an extensive trellised arcade was illuminated with thousands of electric light bulbs, creating a façade for the exhibition hall facing the AEG pavilion. Points of light also traced the outlines of sunken gardens, and a dozen little fountains played under a pergola of white trellis.

The AEG pavilion was opened by the Kaiser himself. He was, of course, a prime mover of the Navy League, the campaign to develop Germany's naval power.[19]

Perhaps it was this building that gave the idea that Behrens might be employed as an architect for the AEG, despite the fact that he was unqualified. At any rate he began to work on more substantial projects for permanent buildings, early in 1908. These were (roughly in order of completion) the re-modelling of a partly built workshop block by the architect Johann Kraaz; a little power-house for the Turbine factory on the Huttenstrasse site in Moabit, and finally the best-known of all his buildings, the new Turbine Factory itself, on the same north-Berlin site.

The power house is a brick building about 16 × 10 metres (52 × 32 ft), not unlike the *Schiffbauausstellung* pavilion in some details, and once again, reminiscent of Ravenna—this time, perhaps, of the mausoleum of Galla Placidia. There is a shallow bay on one side for the switchgear and controls, arched windows coming down to the ground elsewhere, a trapezoid pediment at each end, and nice brick detailing, such as the cornice, the string courses of corrugated brickwork, and the strongly marked voussoirs over the arches. The building contains the dynamos for generating electrical power for the workshops, and is linked to the boiler house with a small lean-to section also designed by Behrens. This generating plant served the large and novel building that has become the symbol of Behrens' industrial works, the *Turbinenhalle*.

With the alteration of the *Alte Fabrik für Bahnmaterial* (the old workshop for railway materials), Behrens began the process of gradually altering and replacing buildings on the Brunnenstrasse site of the AEG which had been designed and executed by his predecessors Schwechten and Kraaz. The *Alte Fabrik* was a five-storey workshop some 87 metres (284 ft) long, with its façade along Voltastrasse, next to two older buildings, a foundry and a die-stamping workshop, by Franz Schwechten (1900). Kraaz had incorporated a good many decorative details from these neighbouring buildings in his Gothic revival design of 1904, notably the vertical emphasis of buttresses, little pinnacles, and a distinctive criss-cross diaper pattern, which he introduced sporadically. The back of the building was designed to have two large wings projecting at right angles in plan, into the main factory terrain.

By 1907, the main block on Voltastrasse and only one of the wings (the east) had been completed. Behrens was charged with adding the second, west, wing and a water tower to the inward side of the workshop. In setting about this, he retained the essential form of the designs by Kraaz, but

AEG factories on the Humbolthain, Berlin.

Old Workshop for Railway Materials, Johann Kraaz; alterations and completion by Behrens, 1908.

simplified them and cut out all the decoration. For the water-tower, he eliminated all the fourteenth century town hall flavour of the original design by Kraaz. This water-tower, with its clock, is not unlike Olbrich's tower, the *Hochzeitsturm*, at Darmstadt, which was then under construction. It is noticeable that Olbrich's work of this period, up to his death in 1908, had also become fundamentally Neo-Classical and geometric, stripped of ornament and soberly restrained. His large exhibition hall on the *Mathildenhöhe* is an example. Several of the other new buildings of that time that were added to the Darmstadt colony were similar to Behrens' contemporary work for the AEG; those by Albin Müller for the 1908 exhibition, for instance.

At the time that Behrens arrived in Berlin, the demand for turbines produced by the AEG was increasing dramatically, as Germany's maritime power developed in rivalry to that of Britain. The engineer Karl Bernhard, with whom Behrens collaborated on the design of the new hall for the *Turbinenfabrik* wrote:

O. Lasche, the factory's director, specified the technical and operational requirements for the new hall. According to him, the contents of the factory's order books in 1904 amounted to only a few thousand horsepower, while by the beginning of October 1909, that is, after scarcely five years of progress, deliveries had already exceeded a million horsepower.

Although the current commercial situation was only moderately favourable, 2,600 men were employed at the factory. The turbo-dynamos and ships' turbines built by the AEG were notable for their economical use of steam, and for their safety of operation.[20]

The factory then producing turbines was much too small—18 metres wide (58 ft)—and it was equipped with cranes that could only lift 25 tons. The new hall was designed to receive material from the railway tracks that branched from a main line some distance away and which came straight into the site and into the rear of the building. Very large turbine engines could then be constructed and moved about the interior of the great new hall on huge travelling gantries, until they were finished. It was decided that these gantries had to have a clear space under them of over 15 metres (49 ft) in height; they also had to have a lifting capacity of 50 tons each, or 100 tons together, and to move such weights at a speed of 2 metres (6 ft) per second. A number of swivelling cranes for moving smaller components and material needed unimpeded room for manoeuvre from the side walls. For all these reasons, a perfectly clear rectangular volume had to be created.

The resultant factory building was the largest steel hall in Berlin at the time, with an enclosed volume of 151,000 cubic metres (197,500 cu yd). Initially 123 metres (402 ft) long, later enlarged to 207 metres (678 ft), and 39·3 metres (123 ft) overall wide, it consists of a main hall 25·60 metres (82 ft) wide, and of virtually the same height, with a secondary two storey hall, 12·93 metres (42 ft) wide, along one side. The lower two-storey hall also has travelling gantries. The upper floor is served by two 10-ton cranes, and the lower by two of 40-ton lifting capacity. There is free communication with the interior of the large hall, so that material can readily be transferred from one to the other. Below the two-storey hall is a basement for storage, changing-rooms and so on.

Behrens determined that the two halls should be distinct from one another from the outside, and ensured this by setting the façade of the smaller section back a little from the main street, Huttenstrasse, compared with the façade of the main hall, and treating it as a separate design. (A perspective of 1908 and an elevation of 1909 both show it advancing in front of the larger hall. In these earlier designs, the façade of the little hall is similar to the bay of the *Kraftzentrale*—the power-house—and a more assertive shape than the façade actually built.)

For the large hall, both Behrens and Bernhard resolved to use fewer, more massive girder frames than might usually have been used for a building on such a scale without internal supports. They wished to make the interior and the exterior as simple as possible in appearance. As Behrens wrote:

(Top) Turbine Hall, Moabit, Berlin, 1909.

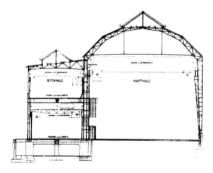

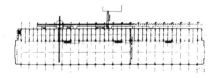

(Left) Turbine Hall: Cross-section (above); Plan (below).

For the construction of the main hall, the overriding architectonic idea was to bring masses of steel together, and not, as is common with the usual lattice constructions, to disperse them everywhere.[21]

The twenty-two great girder frames that form the skeleton of the structure are made up of big box-section steel stanchions on the long Berlichingenstrasse side of the building; the roof structure is of two arched girders joined at their springing with a tie-bar, and meeting at the crest in a bearing surface. The foot of each roof girder on the inner side of the building rests on a corresponding pillar of the side hall: the structure is, therefore, asymmetrical in cross-section. The stanchions along the Berlichingenstrasse side are tapered downwards, and each rests on a bearing surface just above the ground. These hinges or bearing surfaces were believed to be necessary at that period, so that the whole structure might change shape slightly with the expansion and contraction of the component parts when they were exposed to changes of temperature. A famous precedent for a great building of this type was the gigantic *Halle aux Machines* in Paris, constructed for the Exhibition of 1889. Modern practice is usually to omit this provision of links, bearing surfaces or hinges. The *Turbinenhalle* stanchions have, of course, to bear the weight of the travelling gantries and their loads. In a sense the whole building is a rig for travelling cranes, with a roof overhead and windows shielding the sides.

The tapered stanchions are so arranged that the outside surface of the stanchion is vertical, while the inner face slopes inwards as it rises to the springing of the roof. It appears (from Bernhard's account) to have been Behrens' idea to put the windows between each stanchion on the same plane as this inner surface, so that, when viewed from the outside, the great windows slope back at an angle, progressively revealing the thickness of the stanchions as they grow wider towards the top. This device also reveals the full depth of the horizontal girder above them, that links the stanchions together along the whole length of the building. This thickness gives the girder and the supporting stanchions the appearance of a cornice above columns.

The rounded corners of the building are non-load-bearing, and are made of concrete divided by horizontal steel bands. Behrens rationalized their part in the building as follows:

The two corner pillars have only a binding and enclosing function. It is precisely for that reason that they are made of another material, that is to say, concrete; and through their horizontal structure they are in opposition to the verticality of the construction [as a whole]: they play no part in its stability. They are also given the same sloping angle as that shown by the windows.[22]

It is typical of Behrens that he wished thus to counteract one dominant movement in a design with another in opposition to it.

Many observers have felt that these corners (both sides of which slope back in the same plane as the windows, thus having a 'battered' effect) give a heavy, massive and powerful impression, in contradiction to the expressed intention of the architect. They do rather resemble the sloping rusticated masonry of the base of some Renaissance Palazzo; they are not easy to read as a mere skin or filling. They have the appearance of supporting the end gable of the barrel vaulted roof, and this impression, coupled with the outwardly trabeated effect of the long flank of the building, is in reality misleading about the true structural system of the whole.

Although there is no doubt that the success of this building springs from the close collaboration of the architect and the engineer, Karl Bernhard's discussion of the building was, in retrospect, by no means without criticism of the aesthetics of the design. He wrote:

It must be admitted that the grand architectonic effect of the gable, in the light of the effect that was intended—that is, to let the corners stand out only as a cladding, is unfortunate. Everyone sees the gable, which is made of thin reinforced concrete built out from the steel structure, as a heavy concrete construction: two corner pillars and a high pediment. This effect, not foreseen by Prof. Behrens, is such that *Oberbaurat* Erhard in Vienna, in a publication on 'Modern Tectonics', described the Turbine Hall of the AEG as being of 'reinforced concrete', and presents it as an example of a style 'true to materials'. It is a relapse of true artistic endeavour, to envelop the structure of large engineering works in big smooth planes. The steel and glass façade on Berlichingenstrasse is a true and unassailed work of steel constructive art, an artistic success, which is to be doubted of the gable end.[23]

He added warmly elsewhere, that

. . . the artist brought weighty arguments to bear on the engineer, to do other than that which technology simply would have yielded . . . The employment of a reinforced concrete envelope on the gable front, so much discussed in the art world, is objectionable to the author, on grounds of artistic truth.

These criticisms are, of course, typical of those levelled at architects by engineers. They are interesting here particularly because the Turbine Hall has so often been cited as a work of 'frank industrial architecture' in which pure functionalism found its first great twentieth-century expression. It can be seen that Behrens was, rather, imposing his *Kunstwollen* on the factory. (This was a term popularized by Riegl, meaning a desire to impose pattern and meaning on material, independent of technical limitations.)

It has been remarked that the height and width of the hall are more or less identical, so that the façade fits into a square. The curvature of the gable is made up of six equal chords of a circle (also, as Bernhard noted, 'on artistic grounds') 30 metres (98 ft) in diameter. The rectangular part of the façade, comprising the two corner pylons and the great window (which is hung in a vertical plane, flush with the surface of the segmental arch of the pediment) can more or less be inscribed into this circle, suggesting that here, as elsewhere, Behrens was using his favourite geometrical device.

Bernhard wrote that the time allowed for designing the building was very short—from the autumn of 1908 until the spring of 1909, when the construction work (by Czarnikow of Berlin) began (30 March). The foundations took three months to prepare, and the steelwork (carried out by *Dortmund Union*) took only five further months, so that the first 127 metre (415 ft) section was ready in October 1909.

The Turbine Hall, although still to be considered as a landmark in the development of modern architecture, was, of course, by no means a novelty in the sense of being a factory designed as 'architecture', nor in that it was invested with a dramatic, temple-like air. Behrens' desire to make his factory 'sing the great song of work!' (*'Das hohe Lied von Arbeit singen!'*)[24] was not an uncommon ambition among nineteenth-century architects.

Its particular genius lay in the expressive power of steel and glass used on a very large scale, without decorations of any kind; in the carefully related proportions of the building; in the consideration given to each structural feature. The link at the foot of each stanchion is a detail which illustrates this. These pivots have two large steel plates, one at the foot of each stanchion and one on the top of the foundation pier, just above ground level. Each has a vertical flange, between which are hidden the actual load-bearing surfaces, the point at which the stanchion rests on its support. (It is no doubt located on a steel pin driven into both elements). Each of these flanges is stiffened by three curved steel webs. On reflection, it is realized that these webs might have been almost any shape. But their form, their curve, and the exposure of these joints as a whole, suggests power and elasticity—'hingeing'—to our minds. There is a potential for movement implied by these curved webs, like those massive pivots and links of nineteenth-century suspension bridges, that lends a sense of drama to our impression of the whole force of the building being brought down and concentrated on this small point before our eyes, where we can simply touch it.

Critical reception of the Turbinenhalle

Many observers of the art, architecture and industrial design world regarded Behrens' appointment with the AEG as having great significance for the relationship between art and society. His achievements were enthusiastically discussed in print.

The *Werkbund*, an association of artists, designers, craftsmen, academics, political economists and industrialists, had only just been created (October 1907) and Behrens was a founder member. His role within the AEG appeared to be exemplary for the aims of the new organization. As Joan Campbell has written,[25] 'Behrens soon became prominent within the new association. Indeed, his position in the AEG corresponded so closely to the *Werkbund* ideal that he may be regarded as its most representative figure in the pre-war era'. She quotes Julius Posener as referring to Behrens as 'Mr *Werkbund*'. It is not difficult to see how closely the social, national and artistic goals of the *Werkbund* corresponded with those of Behrens.

The *Werkbund* was concerned with the reform of art and design education; with the reconciliation of Fine and Applied Art; with the role of the artist in an industrial society; with exhibition programmes to disseminate good architecture and interior design; with 'the shaping of a culture based on respect for the creative power of the individual personality'; and, what is more, with the expansion of German influence and economic strength in the world. Few members were preoccupied with all these issues, but most were concerned with at least some of them. Hermann Muthesius, who had already influenced Behrens' career, was one if not *the* prime mover of the foundation of the *Werkbund*, as was Friedrich Naumann, the Christian-Socialist liberal politician and political theorist. Naumann regarded the *Werkbund* as comparable with the Navy League: he argued that 'just as the League encouraged Germany to demand a larger role in world politics, so the *Werkbund* should work to extend Germany's economic power'.[26]

Wolf Dohrn, the Executive Director of the *Werkbund* wrote with enthusiasm of his visit to the Turbine Hall:

Whoever has the good fortune to visit the factory receives the strongest impression of a highly individualized spirit in the work inside this many-limbed monster. I will never forget the sight. From the factory office, a door opened on to an elevated gallery, from which one of the technical directors showed me the great hall. He led me into the gigantic factory hall as one might invite someone into a pleasant room. Everything appeared so well arranged, clean and festive in this work hall. And everything open to view. One could see into every last corner. No angles, no dividing walls, no little compartments. Like trees in an avenue, to the right and left of the passageways, which were kept scrupulously clean, were the work stations with their machine tools, and the dynamos, turbines and other machines in course of being built. Internal transportation through the hall is carried out from above in the roof space, by travelling cranes running on tracks. They bring the finished machines to testing rigs under the gallery on which we stand. If they prove to be in order, the travelling crane takes them, lifts them up high and moves with them to the exit. Throughout the entire space, no transmission [chains or belts] interrupts the free movement. There are only individual power units—that is to say, each machine tool has its own motor. In this way it can be brought to the work being undertaken. And the work itself is done in many ways once more like the old methods of handcraftsmanship, in which the tool is taken to the piece of work, and not the work taken to the machine. The equipment has, of course, grown far bigger than that used in handcraftsmanship, and they are not hand, but machine tools. But in the methods of work, the same principle is once more in operation.[27]

It is possible to see Wolf Dohrn's discussion of these issues raised by the Turbine Hall as contributing to the ideas that lay behind the course organization of Gropius's Bauhaus in the 1920s, whereby students were required to work both by hand and with light engineering tools. Electrically powered machinery could be reconciled with the ideals of the Arts-and-Crafts movement. He wrote further:

What refinement such halls may achieve, when engineer and architect go hand in hand! There is such a great, concentrated, powerful feeling to be found in such halls that one can scarcely think of a more wonderful task for the architect, than to give shape with the simplest means to the correct design and arrangement of spaces. It is good, that a new factory building for the AEG will be entrusted to the engineer Bernhard and Peter Behrens, in collaboration. Berlin will have a building in which the technological spirit of our age will find a model, a monument.[28]

Early in 1910, Karl Ernst Osthaus wrote an article describing the building with equal enthusiasm—Behrens considered it to be the best. Osthaus remarked that the only decoration was the monogram AEG and the inscription, 'Turbinenfabrik'. Writing from the point of view of an industrialist's heir, he observed with approval that there were 'no little nooks interrupting the view, where foremen might take a mid-day nap, or hide bungled work. All lies under the eyes of the controller'.[29]

Walter Gropius, who acknowledged the influence of Behrens on his thinking for many years after he left Behrens' office, was surely echoing him when he wrote the text of his brochure Industriebauten—an introduction to a travelling exhibition of photographs which he organized in 1911 for Osthaus's Deutsche Museum für Kunst in Handel und Gewerbe (German Museum for Art in Trade and Commerce). This text sums up so many of the issues surrounding Behrens and the Turbine Hall.

It is not enough, Gropius wrote, to just provide light, air and cleanliness for the factory worker: the worker has a right, no matter how uneducated he may be, to have his native sense of the beautiful awakened. There is also the question of the good publicity to be gained by the employment of artists and architects; the character of the entire undertaking can be expressed to the public by the appearance of the factory. Industry, moreover, which brings so many people together to work collectively, can have an equally powerful influence on the development of a new civilisation as, in the past, the dynastic, individual will of a sovereign used to have.

In all this, Gropius shows himself to be a follower of the ideas of Behrens or Walther Rathenau. He might have been specifically describing the Turbinenhalle itself, however, when he wrote of the energy and economy of modern life as inspiring

Precisely stamped form, in every instance bare [of ornament]: clear contrasts; regular units, symmetrical divisions; unity of form and colour: these establish the foundations of rhythm in modern architectural creation.

He added elsewhere his approval of closed, smooth planes in recent metal construction, as opposed to the old-fashioned lattice type of structure. It may be remarked that the preference for such 'smooth, closed planes' was not only typical of the designs produced at the Bauhaus in the 1920s, but remains a strong characteristic of the German approach to design to this day: the Berlin buses (M.A.N. Type 1975) which pass the Turbinenfabrik every few minutes today possess an obvious family resemblance to Behrens' factory building.

The *Turbinenhalle* is today owned by *Kraftwerk Union*. Since 1956, it has been listed as a protected monument; in 1978 it was partially restored and the exterior given a colour scheme of naples yellow for the concrete and green for the steelwork.

Three major new factories

About the time that the design of the *Turbinenhalle* commenced, Ludwig Mies van der Rohe entered the studio of Behrens. Mies (then aged twenty-two), like Gropius, was employed on the detailing of many of the projects that were handled by the office, both for the AEG and for Behrens' private practice.

On the older factory site by the Humbolthain (a little wooded hill and park in Berlin-Wedding), bounded by Gustav Meyer Allee, Voltastrasse, Hussitenstrasse and Brunnenstrasse, Peter Behrens was required to follow up his modifications to the *Alte Fabrik* with three entirely new buildings.

These three huge factories were designed and constructed between 1909 and 1913. They were the *Hochspannungsfabrik*, for the manufacture of trans-formers, resistors and high-tension components; the *Kleinmotorenfabrik*, a factory for making small motors, and an Assembly Hall for the construction of very large machines, the *Montagehalle für Grossmaschinen.* Behrens also designed an extension to the *Alte Bahnfabrik* on Voltastrasse, on the sites of the old *Metalgiesserei* (foundry) and *Stanzerei* (a die-stamping shop), which were by Franz Schwechten and which were demolished for the new exten-sion. The façade of the *Alte Fabrik* itself was simplified and stripped of its Gothic revival decorative detail in 1911, in order to achieve a unified group of façades along the whole of Voltastrasse, something in the order of 0·4 km ($\frac{1}{4}$ mile) of different buildings. The new buildings were spectacularly big structures in brick, steel and concrete, several of which were again designed in collaboration with the engineer Karl Bernhard.

The first designs for the *Hochspannungsfabrik* appeared in February 1909. The building replaced four single-storey sheds near to the entrance where a branch line from the main railway enters the site, in the north-west corner of the AEG terrain. Behrens' *Hochspannungsfabrik* was obliged to be almost identical in general plan to the old sheds, which had been four long rectan-gular workshops adjacent to one another, but with the ends nearest to the site entrance stepped back progressively in plan to allow for the railway line curving round the building. The increase in accommodation required was obtained by building the new workshop higher. This was done in a novel way—by surrounding two long single-storey sheds on three sides by a six-storey building.

At the four corners of the building are towers containing staircases, lifts and lavatories, and there are lesser staircase towers halfway along the north and south sides.

The east façade of the *Hochspannungsfabrik* is the most powerful and expressive. The gable ends of the central double shed protrude through the six-storey high bridge that links the two outer workshop buildings, and are expressed as two triangular pediments; they are flanked by two great towers. The staircases within the towers are strongly emphasized on the outside by stepped groups of windows in threes, and by the giant steps of the flat roofs of these parts of the towers. The west end is rather less dramatic, as the angle at which the whole façade is laid back tends to destroy the relationship between the towers at this end. The twin pediments also read less well on this side, being partly obscured when seen from the site entrance. Also, Behrens had to sacrifice something of the gigantic stepped effect of the staircase wells at this end, when he revised the plans in 1910 in order to provide better access to the goods lift in the north-west tower.

The *Hochspannungsfabrik* is a steel-framed building clad in brick; the uprights along the flanks of the building are stressed, and given a column-like aspect, as each has a vestigial capital at the top. Over these pillars runs a firm dentilled cornice in brick. The whole building is another expression of Behrens' conviction that the modern movement in art and architecture was developing a new classical art, adapted to the demands of modern times, and in accord with the whole complex of modern conditions. This new classicism depended on simplification and clear proportional relationships: 'Therein is, rather, a simplification in favour of the attempt to have clear proportions in the individual parts, than rich ornamentation'.[30] This was written apropos his arc lamps, but may be taken to represent his approach to architecture as well. The effects of austere massing of form and space are, unfortunately, much more convincing in the preparatory drawings and perspective watercolours than in the fact of the building itself, a familiar disaster in architecture. The building is robbed of a principal façade in the traditional sense by its setting. Whilst the *Turbinenhalle* has a façade and a magisterial flank in the tradition of the temple and the church, the *Hochspannungsfabrik* is not saved by its towers and pediments from being a curiously unmemorable and featureless building.

The next of the Humbolthain buildings, the *Kleinmotorenfabrik*, was designed in 1909 and begun late in 1910. It was built in three sections until completed in 1913. Once more, this building replaced an earlier one which was demolished to make way for it. The whole range of this factory presents a magnificent 196 metre (642 ft) long façade to Voltastrasse, composed of tall half-round columns or piers of purplish-blue engineering bricks supporting a plain, unbroken entablature. The façade is divided into four bays separated by flat pilasters which form a continuous surface with the architrave in such a way that the seven half-round columns in each bay appear to be framed; there is, in this arrangement, an echo of classical columns *in antis*. Each pier has a narrow band of vertical fluting at the top, like a vestigial capital, and each projects from a narrow vertical strip of wall only one and a half bricks wide on either side. Between each of these vestigial walls and

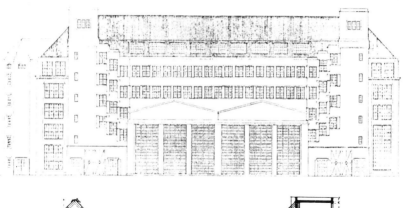

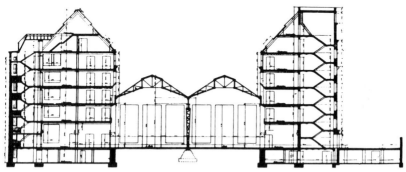

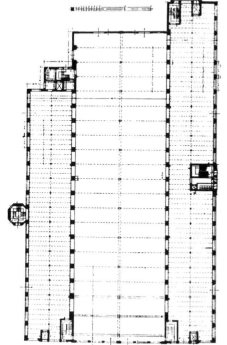

(Opposite) AEG High Tension Materials Factory, Berlin-Wedding, 1910.

(Top) AEG High Tension Materials Factory: Elevation.

(Above) High Tension Materials Factory: Cross-section.

(Left) High Tension Materials Factory: Ground Plan.

The drawings are to different scales.

97

flush with their surface are three bays of steel-framed windows, the mullions of which are painted blueish-green. The horizontal lines of the three floors appear as flat surfaces threading their way behind the columns. The windows of the fifth floor are in a continuous strip, a sort of dormer in the mansard roof; skylights above this illuminate the sixth floor in the roof space.

The inner face of this long building, facing the inside of the industrial site, closely resembles the side elevations of the *Hochspannungsfabrik*, having bays of broad windows four storeys high, and a continuous frieze or attic storey of smaller windows, two above each bay. There are three major projecting wings on this side and a small, faceted staircase tower like that on the south side of the *Hochspannungsfabrik*. But the most effective façade, and one of Behrens' masterpieces, is the great stoa-like range of columns, some 20 metres (65 ft) high, along Voltastrasse. Hoeber wrote that the façade expressed the enormous industrial output of the building—some 10,000 motors each month—while Fritz Mannheimer (in the *Werkbund Jahrbuch* of 1913) compared its impact with that of the vaulting of Gothic cathedrals, or with Paestum or Stonehenge.

The third great building on the site was the *Montagehalle*, an assembly shop for large machines. This was designed in 1911 and built the following year. As planned, this building was about 176 metres (576 ft) long, flanking Hussitenstrasse. Its gable end, to the south, was eventually to occupy the corner and to terminate the whole range of factories on Voltastrasse. (At the time, only thirteen of the projected sixteen bays were constructed, and the corner of the site was not completed until 1928.) Each 10 metre (32 ft) bay was formed, as in the *Turbinenhalle*, by a giant steel girder frame. The raison d'être of the Assembly Hall was also similar, in that it had to support two travelling gantries, each with a capacity of 75 tons suspended above the usual railway branch line that came inside the building. Hussitenstrasse slopes quite strongly down to the corner with Voltastrasse, so the building stands on a high, slightly battered podium. For most of its length along the inner (north-east) flank lies a wing of the L-shaped new *Fabrik für Bahnmaterial*, contiguously with it.

Many observers feel that it is unjustly eclipsed in fame by the slightly smaller *Turbinenhalle*. It is similar in enclosing a great rectangular volume

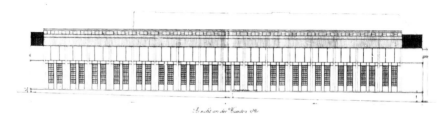

AEG Assembly Hall, Voltastrasse, 1912: Elevation

(Left) AEG Assembly Hall, Voltastrasse, 1912.

(Below) AEG Small Motors Factory, Voltastrasse, 1910.

(Bottom) Small Motors Factory: Elevation; Plan; Inner elevation; Cross-section.

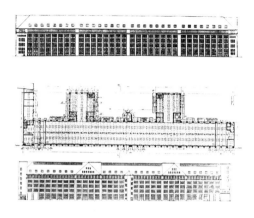

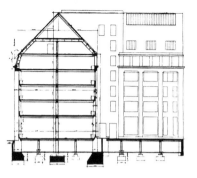

under a multi-faceted roof, but the monumental classicism of the earlier building is less in evidence. The exterior is plain and understated, and there are no ambiguous passages like the heroic concrete pylons and gable of the earlier hall; the windows are hung in a vertical plane between the stanchions, which project very little. The grouping of uprights and horizontals was carefully considered for their proportion and rhythm. Comparisons have been made with Mies van der Rohe's wall systems on the IIT Campus at Chicago (1956).

In addition to these major factory buildings, Behrens prepared several designs (1909–11) for a monumental entrance to the site. This was not built. He also redesigned the roof garden on top of the administrative building (used for receptions in the summer), providing his usual white lattice pergolas and white painted furniture.

The AEG established a complex of factories at Hennigsdorf to the north-west of Berlin (now in the DDR). Between 1910 and 1915, a number of factory buildings designed by Behrens were erected there, on a site situated on the Havel (Hohenzollern) canal, which links Berlin with Stettin (now Szczecin, Poland) and the Baltic sea. They were a porcelain factory, comprising five linked, pitched-roofed sheds, a small brick-built factory for the production of oilcloth, and another for making varnish—all products related to the electrical industry. More impressive was a locomotive works, which was extended between 1913 and 1918 until it was made up of four large interconnected workshops, each rather smaller than, but similar in appearance to the *Montagehalle* on the Humbolthain site. In 1915, a lower, wider group of four such steel-framed halls were constructed, for the manufacture of aircraft.

Hennigsdorf, about 15 km (9 miles) from Berlin, was still a largely country district, so in 1910–11 the AEG built workers' housing in association

AEG Hennigsdorf, Aircraft Assembly Workshop, 1915.

with these new factories. This was Behrens' first introduction to the design of housing for the masses.

During the summer of 1910, Charles Edouard Jeanneret (Le Corbusier) arrived in Behrens' office, where he was to spend five months. Jeanneret,

Apartment houses at Hennigsdorf, 1910–11.

who had been commissioned by his School of Art in La Chaux-de-Fonds to prepare a report on applied art in Germany, was to write of Behrens in 1912:

His most recent factory, the *Turbinenhalle* may be described as a veritable Cathedral of Work. He is building the extensive workers' housing estates in which the community of 150,000 souls, who expect to win their daily bread from the AEG, are to be housed. Behrens is a powerful, profound, serious genius, gripped by an urge to impose control; he is as if created for these tasks and for this time: most congenial to the spirit of present-day Germany.[31]

In fact, Behrens' housing schemes for the AEG were relatively modest in scale. These first apartment houses are pleasant, if unremarkable, three-storey red brick buildings, with attic windows in the steeply sloping roofs. In plan the group forms a 'U' shape facing the main street, Rathenaustrasse. The windows are for the most part generous and grouped in horizontal bands, picked out with white brick architraves and mullions. The 34 units of accommodation vary from two to three-roomed apartments, all with a small lobby, a fair-sized kitchen and a bathroom. At that time, some single rooms were available for lodgers and visitors on a short-term basis. Two shops were provided on the ground floor, on either side of the forecourt, and there were gardens at the back.

Furniture for working-class families, 1912.

Apartment housing at Hennigsdorf: Half-plan.

In connection with these houses, Behrens designed furniture that was exhibited in the spring of 1912 at the Trades Union Headquarters in Berlin. Various periodicals illustrated kitchens, living rooms and bedrooms designed by Behrens for working-class families.[32]

Behrens also designed a little boathouse at Hennigsdorf for those employees who were rowing enthusiasts.

In a diametrically opposite direction from the centre of Berlin, at Oberschöneweide (today in East Berlin) the AEG developed another group of factories in the south-east, on the bank of the river Spree. This group included a cable works, a rubber works and a motor-car factory. The new factory for the NAG (*Nationale*, formerly *Neue*, *Automobil AG*), a subsidiary of the AEG, was designed in 1915 and built the following year. The site was trapezoidal in plan (on the corner of Wilhelminenhofstrasse and Ostendstrasse, very close to the river), and the seven-storey workshops built around the perimeter of the site enclose two long single-storey pitched-roofed sheds on three sides, horseshoe fashion, rather in the manner of the *Hochspannungsfabrik*. The entrance to the offices is through an arch at the foot of a 70 metre (229 ft) high tower; the reception hall is a severe arcaded space reached from below: the flight of steps from the entrance comes up into the middle of the floor. A feature of the exterior of all the buildings of this complex is the heavy stepped cornice projecting at an angle of about 45°.

The NAG factory, which produced cars and lorries, is today an electronics works for the manufacture of television components (*VEB Werk für Fernsehelektronik*).

Between 1911 and 1915, a really big garden city for the AEG workers at Oberschöneweide was planned by Behrens. This is perhaps the plan referred to by Jeanneret and other contemporaries. Plans and elevations are in existence which show groupings of four-storey apartment blocks with balconies and terraces around garden courts, all relating to this scheme: what would now be described as 'low rise, high density' housing. What was in fact carried out in 1915 was a modest scheme of 170 dwellings, mostly small two-storey terraced houses with additional attic bedrooms with dormer windows. Each house had a 'utility room'. These were built on the site of the ambitious scheme referred to above, between Zeppelinstrasse, Roedernstrasse, An der Wulheide and Fontanestrasse. The houses are rendered in grey cement, the windows have shutters, and the central plot of ground is given over to gardens and allotments.

A little earlier, Behrens designed, as at Hennigsdorf, a boathouse for employees. It was opened in May 1912. This was a substantial building, as the members of the Elektra rowing club were drawn largely from the engineers and salesmen of the staff of the AEG and the BEW. The three-storey building by the water's edge, containing a boathouse, a dining-room, changing room and dormitory, still stands today.

An AEG factory was built in Riga (Latvia) in 1913. It appears to have been closely modelled on the *Hochspannungsfabrik*, but with a single tower, much taller than those of the earlier, Berlin factory.

Notes

1. P. J. Cremers, *Peter Behrens, Sein Werk von 1909 bis zur Gegenwart*, Essen, Baedecker, 1928.
2. Letters from Peter Behrens of 31 December 1905 and 11 February 1906 to Maximilian Harden, now in the Bundesarchiv, Koblenz (*Signatur* No. 9) establish the

earliest yet known contact between Behrens and Rathenau. I am indebted to Frau Hedwig Singer of the Bundesarchiv for her help in finding these letters.

3. Letter No. 52, Walther Rathenau, *Briefe: Neue Folge*, Dresden, Reissner, 1928, p106. It has been remarked that Rathenau's political and economic writings, if frequently incoherent and self-contradictory, were a blueprint for the kind of social organization Behrens was consciously helping, as architect and designer, to create.
4. Osthaus Archiv, Kü 416. Dated 31 July 1907.
5. *Werkkunst*, Yr. 2, No. 22, August 1907, p351, and in the *Berliner Tageblatt* of 28 July 1907.
6. The Spanish artist, Fortuny, designed and patented a lighting system for the theatre, which was produced by the AEG from October 1906. See *Immagini e materiale del Laboratorio Mariano Fortuny*, Venice, Museo Fortuny, 1978. Behrens designed a catalogue for this system in 1908.
7. Walter Gropius, *Apollo in der Demokratie*, Mainz, Florian Kupferberg, 1967, pp124–5.
8. And yet again, Max Hertwig, a draughtsman with Behrens, maintained that Gropius started in June 1908. See Herta Hesse-Frielinghaus et al, *Karl Ernst Osthaus* op. cit., p504 n6.
9. *Werkkunst* Yr. 2, No. 24, September 1907, p382.
10. Peter Behrens, 'Zur Ästhetik des Fabrikbaus', *Gewerbefleiss* Yr. 108, No. 7/9, July/Sept 1929.
11. Fritz Hoeber, *Peter Behrens* op. cit., p221.
12. Buddensieg, T. and Rogge, H., 'Formgestaltung für die Industrie: Peter Behrens und die Bogenlampen der AEG', *Von Morris zum Bauhaus: Eine Kunst gegründet auf Einfachkeit*, ed. Bott, G. op. cit.
13. A letter of 5 June 1958 in Helmut Weber, *Walter Gropius und das Faguswerk*, Munich, Callwey, 1961, p23.
14. See the illustration of Behrens' living room in Berlin in P. J. Cremers op. cit., p121.
15. Franz Mannheimer, '*Arbeiten von Prof. Peter Behrens für die AEG Berlin*', *Der Industriebau*, II, 15 June 1911, p124.
16. Wolf Dohrn, '*Das Vorbild der AEG*', *März* III, 3 Sept 1909.
17. Peter Behrens in *Gewerbefleiss* op. cit.
18. Letter from Walter Gropius to Helmut Weber, in Weber, *Faguswerk* op. cit.
19. M. Balfour, *The Kaiser and His Times*, London, Penguin, 1975.
20. Karl Berhard, '*Die neue Halle für die Turbinenfabrik der AEG*', *Zeitschrift des Vereines deutscher Ingenieure* 55, No. 38, 30 Sept 1911, pp1625–31; 1673–82.
21. Peter Behrens, '*Die Turbinenhalle der AEG zu Berlin*', *Mitteilungen des Rheinischen Vereins für Denkmalpflege und Heimatschutz* Yr. 4, No. 1, 1 March 1910, pp26–9.
22. Ibid.
23. Karl Berhard, *Die neue Halle . . .* op. cit.
24. Professor A. Hoff, *Peter Behrens, Persönlichkeit und Werk*. Henry van de Velde Gesellschaft, Hagen, 1966.

25. Joan Campbell, *The German Werkbund: The politics of reform in the applied arts*, Princeton, 1978.
26. Joan Campbell, op. cit.
27. Wolf Dohrn, *Das Vorbild der AEG* op. cit.
28. Ibid.
29. Karl Ernst Osthaus, *'Ein Fabrikbau von Peter Behrens'*, *Frankfurter Zeitung*, 10 February 1910.
30. Peter Behrens, *'Über Ästhetik in der Industrie'*, *AEG-Zeitung*, June 1909, pp5–12.
31. Ch. E. Jeanneret (Le Corbusier), *Étude sur le mouvement d'art décoratif en Allemagne*, La Chaux de Fonds, Haefeli, 1912.
32. See Hoeber, *Peter Behrens*, op. cit. LIT. 156a–158 for further reading.

7 Neo-Classical Themes, 1907–14

Domestic Housing

In 1906, Karl Ernst Osthaus decided to free the apartment in the Folkwang Museum that he and his young family had been occupying, so that the rooms might be used for exhibition purposes. He bought a tract of land on a hilltop at Eppenhausen above Hagen, and set about planning a new house for himself, that might be the centre of a garden suburb, or an artists' colony—an idea no doubt inspired by his memory of the *Künstlerkolonie* in Darmstadt. Although at this period he was finding important projects for Behrens in and around Hagen, Osthaus was still very interested in the architecture of Henry van de Velde, and when he considered the design of his proposed housing estate, he chose Van de Velde as the architect of his own house (*Hohenhof*), and divided the terrain into three zones, asking Behrens, Van de Velde and, eventually, the Dutch architect, J. L. M. Lauweriks, to design related groups of houses for these areas, independent of one another, but following a general overall plan.

The 20 h (50 acres) of land at Eppenhausen are in the form of a gentle dome, fairly flat and wooded; the land slopes very steeply away on the north and east sides, and there is a narrow road, hardly more than a track in places, the *Stirnband* (Headband), encircling the crest of the hill. As early as October 1906, Behrens appears to have sent Osthaus a site plan for the whole estate, and a plan of his of 1907 includes a number of large public buildings centred on a square piazza, the so-called *Goldene Pforte* (Golden Gate). One of these projected buildings, a large pedimented building on the east side of the square, straddling the path of the *Stirnband*, was almost certainly to be a new Folkwang Museum. Osthaus, evidently undecided for some years about the division of responsibilities between his three architects, invited the other two at various points to provide solutions to the planning of this cultural centre. There is a plan of the site by Van de Velde of 1906–7 showing the projected new museum as being one of *his* buildings,[1] and another of 1907 which includes some of Behrens' houses, but with different ground plans to those actually built.[2] A further site plan of January 1910 also exists, over which a united sequence of buildings, drawn by Lauweriks in conté crayon, goes right across the whole site, showing his own related group of houses in the positions they occupy today, but also incorporating or replacing buildings allotted elsewhere to either Behrens or Van de Velde.

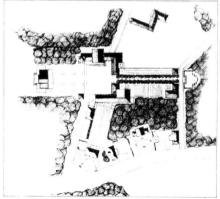

Hohenhagen Garden Suburb, Eppenhausen: Plan, 1907.

The 1907 plan by Behrens is rigid and axial. The buildings around the *Goldene Pforte* are so arranged as to suppress the irregular oblique direction of the *Stirnband* across the square as much as possible. He also planned a straight axis through the square, terminated in the north by a pedimented building approached by a broad formal garden in three shallow terraces; to the south, the avenue *Unter Kastanien* (Under the Chestnut Trees) produces this axis to an open-air theatre. A group of villas on Hassleyerstrasse face a communal rectangular formal garden. The house for Dr Cuno is on an axis of

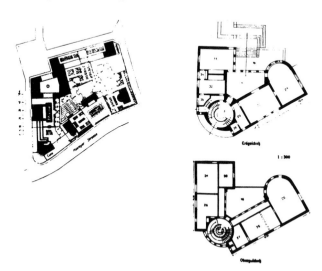

(Left) Hohenhagen Garden Suburb, Eppenhausen: Plan, 1906–7. (Right) Cuno House, earlier plan from Hugo Licht: Ground plan (above); Upper floor (below).

107

its own, facing the corner of Hassleyerstrasse and the *Stirnband*. Hoeber mentions that the Cuno house was earlier planned by Behrens as a building with two wings on either side of a round staircase hall. An idea of this design is given by a plan of Behrens' showing this version of the Cuno house.[3] (Van de Velde's second drawing shows it with an oval room in the middle.) If he had carried out this earlier version, it would have made an emphatic pivot for the corner, and there would have been a related sequence of houses, with movement implied from one to the other across the spaces between them in the manner suggested by Lauweriks (and indeed carried out by him, in the short section of the *Stirnband* with which he was eventually concerned).

The first house of the garden suburb to be started, however, was Behrens' Schroeder house; designed in 1908, it was built the following year. Behrens' houses were not designed for artists. Schroeder was a dentist, Dr Willy Cuno was the Mayor of Hagen, and Goedecke, the local government building inspector. (The artists and musicians attracted to Hagen by

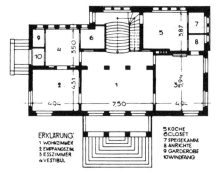

ERKLÄRUNG:
1 WOHNZIMMER
2 EMPFANGSZM.
3 ESSZIMMER
4 VESTIBÜL
5 KOCHE
6 CLOSET
7 SPEISEKAMM.
8 ANRICHTE
9 GARDEROBE
10 WINDFANG

(Above) Schroeder House, Eppenhausen, 1909.

(Left) Schroeder House: Plan.

Osthaus lived in Lauweriks' houses.) The Schroeder house was the third of Behrens' career, and the first to be severely geometrical throughout. It was also the first of his houses to have a living room very much bigger than the dining-room, and this took a central place on the axis of the house, like the hall in a Palladian villa. This room was divided by a screen of pillars that lay directly in line with those of the white portico of the south façade. Behind the screen rose a broad, monumental staircase. This staircase was contained on the north façade of the house in a tower crowned with a semi-circular gable, and was lit by another Palladian feature, a three-light lunette window.

The exterior elevation was in two storeys, the lower being smooth ochre-coloured rendering relieved by the broad brilliant white stone architraves of the doors and windows. The upper storey was narrower, and hung with grey-blue slates above a broad white horizontal band of artificial stone. The regularly placed windows were shuttered, and the pitch of the roof just about 45°. The staircase tower and a balcony were built, by way of contrast, of the local grey limestone as coursed rubble. This stone, quarried on the estate, was used by all three architects as a unifying feature of the houses of the garden suburb.[4]

The Cuno house (1909–10) resembles the Schroeder house in plan, with a big living room and a staircase forming the centre of the house, but the plan is even more symmetrical and rigid. The rectangular rooms on either side of the living room are identical, and the large study for the master of the house is square. As Hoeber wrote shortly after the house was built, 'The distribution of the ground plan is of a unique symmetrical beauty, which in miniature compares with the strict villa plans of an Andrea Palladio . . .'[5]

The exterior is given a little asymmetrical rhythm, typical of Behrens, by the arrangement of the balconies on either side of the building; the one on the right-hand side is wrapped around part of the principal façade as a thick buttressing wall in coursed rubble. The front elevation is indeed a web of evenly balanced vertical and horizontal tensions giving a first impression of symmetry that is only slowly realized to be an illusion. There is a high rusticated base of coursed rubble in the usual local stone, one storey high, above which the walls are rendered smooth. They are topped all round with a thin, flat but emphatic cornice. A similar flat cornice, like an exaggerated string course divides the building half way up. Originally, (and now in its newly restored condition in 1980) the lower section of the rendered walls, between the top of the stone base and this halfway mark was painted white, and the principal wall surface above was painted in a darker tone. Between the upper cornice and the eaves of the roof was a kind of ribbed parapet, stepped back in an unusual way so that the roof did not in fact overhang the walls. This has also recently been restored, following damage due to water penetration.

The garden front is symmetrical, with the three windows of the living room recessed between the projecting stone walls of the rooms on either

side; these walls extend around the sides of the house to support the balconies on either side.

The most striking feature of the main, street façade of the house—the glazed tower containing the spiral staircase, so curiously recessed within the plane of the façade—owes its existence in this form to the abandoned scheme to make the house in two wings meeting at an acute angle. That idea was, incidentally, either a version of the plan of Van de Velde's *Hohenhof* or an echo of an early nineteenth-century Neo-Classical building well known to Behrens, the Kasino by Georg Moller (of about 1817), a landmark of Darmstadt. The two wings of that house had identical smooth flat façades above a rusticated base, and where they met, the corner was effected with a cylindrical tower with four slender pilasters and a canopy above the ground floor. The roof of this tower, like that of the Cuno house, was also kept level with the low-pitched roof of the whole building.

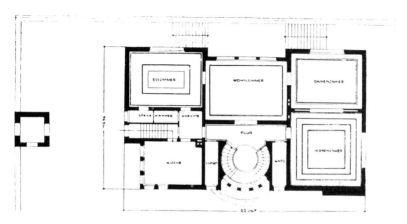

Cuno House, Eppenhausen, 1910, opposite; and (above) Ground plan (final).

As it stands, the Cuno house is an elegant and commanding Palladian villa. It is, nevertheless, not an effective hinge for the corner on which it stands, or a continuation of the line of houses that stood along Hassleyerstrasse. The hinge was, as it were, opened out flat in the change of plan, almost concealing the pivot (the staircase) in the process. It is to this that it owes its tension, its formidably taut and compact appearance; and yet it cannot ever have been a wholly satisfactory house, aesthetically or practically. The design was a contraction of one that would have boldly 'turned' the corner site; but the staircase tower, the canopy and the garden layout in their realized form are not enough to do this; there is no satisfactory spatial relationship with the corner, and it is unlikely that there ever was with the neighbouring Schroeder house either, although Behrens continued to consider it the functional pivot of his scheme.

In terms of practical convenience there were severe disadvantages. The living room faces east-north-east, and, as the house is on the very edge of its site, there is no worthwhile view from it, nor any privacy outside in the garden. The narrow terrace outside the living room directly overlooks other property. The side balconies offer equally little owing to the close proximity of the boundaries of the site. The largest arc of garden is at the front of the house, semi-public and impersonal.

The house also gave a good deal of trouble during and after construction. Although the Schroeder and Cuno houses were expensive (according to Alfred Lichtwark, the Schroeder house cost 40,000 marks, which was more than the original estimate, and the Cuno house cost 100,000 marks), there were technical faults that were the subject of an almost continuous exchange of letters between Osthaus and Behrens over the next two or three years. Lichtwark (Curator of the Hamburg *Kunsthalle*) spotted some of the dangers on his visit in 1910:

Behrens, quite unmistakably. Yes, Yes. But. One can say that even when looking at a half-built house. With Behrens I always first of all see the false starts. Now he has set back the upper floor of one of his villas two hands breadth. The wall of the ground floor makes a corner with that of the first floor: to see that makes me really uneasy. To make a plausible argument for the necessity of this on formal grounds is impossible to my mind. And then there is building practice. What sort of material holds it up? We have such things as rain, snow and frost. Next year, they'll have to make a slope on this salient ledge, and that will look comic. There are things like that all over Van de Velde's work as well. They're walking on their hands.[6]

Following some eye-opening criticisms from a group of visiting architects, Osthaus himself began to be anxious about the two houses:

No matter how much fault should be attached to the way in which the work is carried out, for all that, scandal about the facts of your building supervision will inevitably get about, which will make it very difficult for my plans for further work of yours to be carried out on your intended section of the land. It is not only a matter of the most vexatious dampness of the walls—over which your method is in question, not only in the stepping-back of the walls over the ground floor, but also in the apparently doubtful quality of the artificial stone. The stone must be very porous to let damp through and to fail to withstand frost . . . I would strongly urge you, concerning these troubles, to hand out the sharpest reprimands on Schroeder's behalf, or the group who know of the lamentable neglect of the crematorium and who stir up real animosity, will join the chorus.[7]

Behrens was, of course, frantically overworked and a long way from Hagen most of the time. The exchange of letters between him and Osthaus developed into a lugubrious saga of elementary failures of the kind that give architects and their clients nightmares. These varied from trivial details to alarming structural defects. For example, whilst Osthaus particularly admired Behrens for his method of co-ordinating the dimensions of all the detailed elements of a room, he was obliged to write in December 1910:

A few days ago, in Frau Cuno's living room, I saw that the edges of the carpet have been stuck down without reference to the rectangular divisions of the floor. This arrangement is really annoying, as one doesn't know whether to arrange the furniture in relation to the floor or the walls. In either case a poor effect results. I can't think that this arrangement was intended by you, although I'm not in a position to exactly pin down who is to blame . . .[8]

Throughout the summer of 1910 there was trouble with the circular staircase of the Cuno house, necessitating revised drawings and long letters of explanation from Behrens in Berlin. The discovery of snags dragged on as late as 1913, and throughout, Frau Cuno played a lively part in raising objections and complaints:

Dear Friend!

This morning I once more had the pleasure of being confronted by Frau Cuno. Every time it rains, there is a pool in front of her front door, caused by rain splashing down from the circular canopy. It is imperative that we collect the large amount of water on the edge of the lower roof projection (right over the house door) in a gutter and lead it away down one side. As it is people stand right under the drops when they have to wait for the door to be opened. Then there is the question to be solved of how we can ensure that people have dry feet when at the front door. A mat, with holes in it, if high enough, would be useful to keep one above the level of the puddle, but it would be better—for the house as well—if a slight gradient away from the spot could be created. I must ask you, though, not to lose sight of considerations of the expense . . .[9]

It is never quite clear, in the letters from Osthaus, just how far he was being sarcastic.

The third of Behrens' Eppenhausen villas, the house for Goedecke (1911–12), has attracted less attention in architectural histories than the Schroeder and Cuno houses. Osthaus took the precaution of warning Behrens against structural complications in the design: 'I strongly advise that above all the walls and the roof should be as simple and solid in construction as possible'.[10]

Letters in the Osthaus Archiv show that Goedecke knew exactly what he wanted, how much he would pay and where the house was to be sited. He suggested using a different architect if he could not have what he wanted. He got his own way. No doubt his professional familiarity with building matters helped a great deal; he got the most satisfactory, if the least interesting house from an aesthetic point of view. It appears to have been the least expensive for its size, it was built without recorded hitches, and has a pleasant relationship with its setting. It is a plain house that could easily be mistaken for an eighteenth-century rectory, L-shaped in plan, built on a corner site near to the projected open-air theatre, deeply wooded and far enough away from the road. The roof has firmly overhanging eaves.

The houses in Hagen were a principal source of friction between Behrens

113

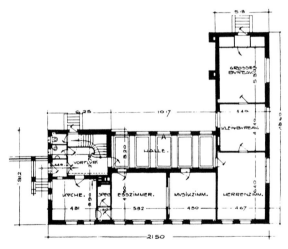

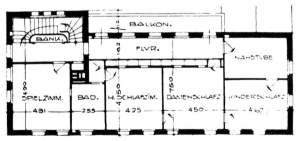

(Above) Goedecke House, Eppenhausen, 1911–12, garden side.

(Left) Goedecke House: Ground plan (top) and Upper floor (bottom).

The drawings are to different scales.

and his brilliant assistant Walter Gropius, and quarrels over them precipitated the departure of Gropius from Behrens' office.

During this period Gropius was responsible for virtually all the detailing and supervision of the Schroeder and Cuno houses. As he recalled: 'In the first phase, wholly in the spirit of Behrens, I had an active share in the Schroeder and Cuno houses, which I saw through in detail almost entirely by myself.'[11] Gropius visited Hagen a number of times in connection with the houses, and consolidated his friendship with Osthaus. By March 1910, however, he was anxious to make his position over the teething troubles of these houses clear to Osthaus. In a long letter to him concerning the defects of the Cuno house he wrote:

. . . on certain points however my influence and my powers of persuasion have proven unavailing, and yet I have, as one of the firm, to defend Behrens' wishes to people outside, against my better judgement.

I'm glad to be able to illustrate my proposals with sketches and letters, as latterly differences between Behrens and myself have so escalated that yesterday I was obliged to see that I can do no further work with him. I would be very happy if you would offer me an early opportunity to discuss these, to me very aggravating matters, with you in person. I can't help being afraid that you may have my role pictured to you in a false light by the other side, and it would be particularly painful to me to be wrongly judged by you . . .[12]

If it was difficult for Osthaus to determine who was to blame for the shortcomings of the houses at the time, in 1910, it is impossible for us to know precisely now. But it is worth remembering that these houses, the fruit of collaboration between two such distinguished architects and reproduced without adverse critical comment in dozens of histories of modern architecture, were failures in many respects. The elementary mistakes over waterproofing and so on remind one that Behrens was self-taught as an architect, and that most of his experience had been with temporary buildings for exhibitions.

Ambitious subordinates found Behrens difficult to work with at that time. Jeanneret described him as *'tragique et déséquilibré'* ('tragic and unstable') in a letter to Osthaus in 1912.[13] Where Gropius's departure is concerned, however, it must be remembered that Gropius was ambitious and arrogant and already, at twenty-six, considered himself very much as in the same league as Behrens, and this may have given cause for resentment. After all, he had, in the same month as his letter quoted above, presented his 'memorandum' on low-cost housing for workers to the industrialist Emil Rathenau.[14] Whether this memorandum was solicited or not is not known, but Rathenau, as head of the AEG, was Behrens' patron in the final analysis. There may also have been the question of Gropius supplanting Behrens in Osthaus's favour, coupled with the relentless stream of unpleasant letters Behrens himself was receiving. Gropius mentioned much later in life that Osthaus intended to commission some houses from him after he had left

Behrens, and that he vaguely remembered doing some drawings for them.[15] When Gropius left Behrens in June 1910, another of the assistants, Adolf Meyer, went with him to become his partner.

The building of the Eppenhausen Garden Suburb came to a halt with the outbreak of the First World War. Afterwards the chances of further development were reduced by the transformation of the financial, political and architectural scenes. The architects were scattered; Lauweriks in Holland, Van de Velde in Switzerland and Behrens in Berlin. In 1921, Karl Ernst Osthaus died. The collection of the Folkwang Museum was sold to Essen, and no more artistic enterprises of interest were undertaken in Hagen for thirty years.[16]

Neuss: The Catholic Community House

In 1907, the *Katholische Gesellenverein* of Neuss (on the Rhine near Düsseldorf) organized a limited competition for a new hostel and community centre, inviting Behrens, Richard Riemerschmid and Paul Schultze-Naumburg to prepare schemes for which Theodor Fischer (the Munich architect) was to be adjudicator. Riemerschmid withdrew and Behrens was chosen.

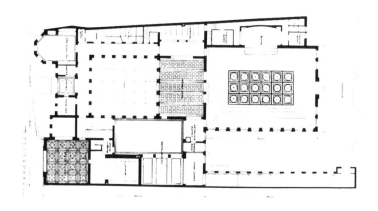

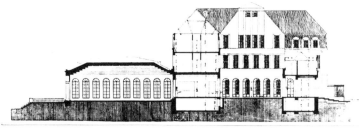

Catholic Community House, Neuss, 1908–10: Section and Plan.

The *Gesellenverein* was a Catholic Journeymen's Association or Working Men's Union which had been founded in 1852, as a branch of the oldest established working men's association in Germany, with a religious rather than a political aim. The *Gesellenhaus* was built between 1909 and the spring of 1910. It incorporates a hostel, a chapel (for which Thorn-Prikker later painted a fresco), a refectory and dining-room, administrative offices and a very large hall for meetings and entertainments. A stage opens on to the latter along one side. There are many details—a pergola, arched arcades and so on—in common with the Eppenhausen villas.[17]

Over a large trapezoidal site (on the north-east corner of which the *Gesellenhaus* was built) was to have been an associated housing estate of an urban character. Arranged around a little piazza and little parks and gardens were to have been apartment houses of two or three storeys for rental by the Association. This interesting scheme, designed in 1910, was never built. The units of accommodation varied between five and six-room apartments on two storeys around courtyards. The perspective drawings show formal but varied groups of buildings with many features in common with the Eppenhausen villas. Although asymmetrically arranged, the classical flavour is strongly reminiscent of Moller's early nineteenth-century Darmstadt.

The Kröller House

A curious episode was the creation of a full-sized mock-up in wood and canvas, on site, of a very large house for the art collectors Anton and Hélène Kröller at the Hague in Holland. In March 1911, they had visited Hagen to see the new houses there for themselves, and at Behrens' request Osthaus met them and showed them round. Later in the year Mies van der Rohe was allotted the task of supervising this design and the erection of a model. The model and Behrens' drawings for the house show it to have been a long, low flat-roofed two-storey building with a large conservatory and internal garden courtyards. After a year, during which Mies spent much time on the project, Mme Kröller invited Mies to prepare an alternative design of his own, and another full-scale model. In the event, this was not accepted either. Finally, the Kröllers used H. P. Berlage as architect.

After the war, Henry van de Velde designed the Kröller-Müller museum at Otterlo; according to Osthaus, the Kröllers had been very impressed by *Hohenhof* during their visit to Hagen.

The Wiegand House

The most important private house of this period, and one of the best known of his career, was the house by Behrens for Dr Theodor Wiegand in Berlin.[18]

Theodor Wiegand (1864–1936) was one of the most distinguished of German archaeologists. He was in charge of the excavations at Priene from 1896, after the death of Carl Humann, and he led further important campaigns elsewhere in Asia Minor: at Milet, Didyma and Samos. Today,

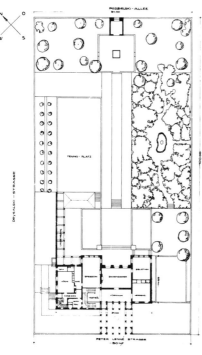

(Above) Wiegand House, Dahlem, 1911–12: Peristyle.

(Left) Wiegand House, Dahlem: Plan.

material from these sites forms a prominent part of the magnificent collection in the Pergamon Museum in Berlin. In 1910, he was made Director of Antiquities of the Royal Prussian Museums, and so was obliged to find somewhere to live in Berlin. It is possible that he chose Behrens as his architect through the intercession of a friend in common, Edmund Schüler. Schüler was attached to the German Embassy in Constantinople, where he knew Wiegand. He claimed to have been instrumental in securing Behrens, about the same time, for the design of the German Embassy in St Petersburg (following, he said, a pilgrimage to the AEG factories, which made him determined to persuade his superiors to employ Behrens for that prestigious commission.).[19]

It is most likely that Dr Wiegand took a close hand in the design of his house. It is the only one of Behrens' houses to take Neo-Classicism as far as the use of Doric columns and pilasters.

The house was built between 1911 and 1912 on a plot of land measuring 50 × 100 metres (164 × 328 ft) between Podbielskiallee and Peter-Lenné-Strasse in Dahlem, one of the most attractive residential areas of Berlin. The house is set far back from the main road, Podbielskiallee, so that the principal entrance is on the quieter Peter-Lenné-Strasse. This entrance is gained through one of the most remarkable features of the house—a peristyle, square in plan, of unfluted Doric columns. On the street front this peristyle has two little corner porches on either side so that the whole feature functions as a forecourt and a propylaeum in one. (Its appearance recalls the entrance Behrens designed for the *Tonhaus Flora* in Cologne in 1906.)

In plan the house has similarities with the Cuno villa; the dining-room is to the left of the entrance hall, the library and study to the right; the large reception room is in the centre, straight ahead. The rooms on either side of the living room project slightly as wings onto the garden front. The house is substantially bigger, however, as not only is this central core larger in length and breadth by several metres than that of the Cuno house, but the spaces are allowed to be more generous, as the kitchen, cloakroom and other offices are additions outside the ground plan described. The staircase also takes up relatively less room.

All five bays of the peristyle have double doors that may be opened into the entrance hall; a provision no doubt for the reception of guests on formal occasions: the arrangement (with a double door opening on the central axis into a large reception room) is reminiscent of Hellenistic town houses of the late fourth century BC, like those Wiegand was responsible for excavating at Priene.[20]

On the first floor are bedrooms and a family living room directly over the more formal reception room of the ground floor. Above the kitchen is a guest bedroom and bathroom. In the roof are servants' quarters.

The whole of the exterior of the house (like the unusually monumental antique houses of Priene) is executed in finely jointed ashlar, using grey shelly limestone. The lower half of the wall is battered with a gently curving profile. The roof (for which one of Behrens' designs shows a Schinkelesque zinc covering) is of red roman tiles.

A covered walk or pergola, beautifully articulated with the house, leads from the dining-room to a rectangular open pavilion overlooking the garden and a tennis court.

Throughout the house there are classical details which, while showing evidence of scholarship, are derived from different periods and are often put together in a deliberately unorthodox way so that the classicism is original and creative within the spirit of Hellenistic domestic architecture. The unorthodoxies are ones that might be found at Priene or Delos. The most striking example of this is in the peristyle. The unfluted Doric columns, without entasis, carry a very simple (basically Ionic) entablature: a plain architrave, no frieze and a cornice resting on a fat echinus moulding. The peristyle incidentally is roofed with glass blocks. Elsewhere Behrens drew on Schinkel, a predecessor who could design from 'inside the skin' of a classical architect. Fritz Neumeyer points out the close resemblance of the whole garden front of the Wiegand house to Schinkel's 1826 design for a town house with a pillared court, and the resemblance of the peristyle to that designed by Schinkel, if differently positioned.

Both Gropius, (in *Apollo in der Demokratie*) and Mies van der Rohe, spoke later of Behrens' enthusiasm for Schinkel and for classical proportion. Gropius wrote:

He led me to the systematic design procedures of the medieval masons' guilds and the geometrical rules of Greek architecture. We often visited buildings by Schinkel in and around Potsdam. In Schinkel he saw his artistic ancestor.

Edwin Redslob, the art historian, recalled Behrens re-erecting parts of a demolished Schinkel house at his Neubabelsberg home.

The Wiegand house was decorated and furnished with meticulous attention to detail. Everything was sober, formal, sumptuous and rather heavy. Behrens displayed his usual prolific virtuosity in the wide range of furniture he designed for the house: kitchen, garden, bathroom, drawing room, dining-room, bedroom and built-in furniture. For some of the accessories, the casing of a central heating radiator is an example—he resurrected a favourite motif, a chariot wheel with Ionic voluted spokes (used earlier in furniture for the Schroeder house.) A similar motif was used ('a graceful reminder of the Palace of Troy') for the bronze doors of the main entrance, and yet again in his St Petersburg Embassy; perhaps Behrens also noticed the motifs below the windows of Schinkel's *Schloss Charlottenhof*. The square-in-a-circle, another favourite motif, is used for the metal grille on top of radiator casings. Elsewhere rosettes were used on built-in cupboards, and the furniture of the principal bedroom has an elaborate palmette design adapted from an Apulian painted amphora.

Today the Wiegand house is the headquarters of the German Archeological Institute. It was lavishly restored in 1978.

The additions and modifications to the house of Frau Dr Mertens (a garage, pergola, tennis court of 1909–10, and some interiors of 1910) had also been taking Behrens to work adjacent to a Schinkel house, in the heart of Neo-Classical Potsdam. About this time, Behrens was asserting that he did not see Morris, Burne-Jones, etc, and what he called 'the similar German romantics' as the pioneers of the modern movement in architecture and design, but rather the nineteenth-century German Neo-Classicists.[21]

The German Embassy, St Petersburg, 1911–12

As previously mentioned, Edmund Schüler (a member of the Foreign Office in 1911) later wrote that he had been responsible for convincing his superior, the Secretary of State, Alfred von Kiderlen-Wächter, that Behrens should be invited to submit a design for the new Embassy in St Isaaks Platz, St Petersburg.

Once invited, Behrens had only eight weeks in which to prepare drawings, but they were delivered on time. They were approved by the authorities concerned, including the Kaiser, and the building commenced. Mies van der Rohe was appointed to supervise the erection and completion of the project.

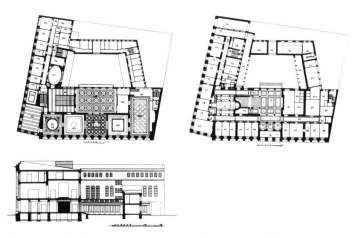

German Embassy, St Petersburg, 1911–12: Ground plan (above right), Upper floor plan (top left), and Cross section.

The site was on the corner of St Isaaks Platz and the Morskaja, one of the principal streets of the city: a rough parallelogram in shape. The square had been enlarged, in 1910, by the clearance of a good many older buildings (against a fair amount of indignant opposition) and gardens laid out in their place.[22]

Behrens had to provide the services of what is, in effect, a town palace. The building had to fit into an urban setting of fine eighteenth and

121

German Embassy, St Petersburg: Perspective.

nineteenth century *palazzi* and, of course, to stand as a symbol of Germany in the eyes of foreigners.

The reception rooms form a large three-storey block with the main, memorable, façade towards the square. At an acute angle to this, a three-storey block flanks the Morskaja, containing offices, the apartments of the Ambassador and his Chancellor, and guest rooms. Together, these blocks form an L-shape in plan. Behrens enclosed a courtyard between the arms of this L-shape with a low two-storey garage and stable range, also L-shaped in plan, so that the courtyard is a regular trapezoid on the central axis of the main building.

The main entrance has three doors, and leads into a great hall. Directly across the hall is the entrance to the courtyard. The main staircase rises at right angles to the axis of the hall, on the left.

On the first floor are the throne room, the dining hall and, along the front of the building, a suite of reception rooms, each square in plan. In the private wing of the Embassy there is a second, oval dining-room for everyday use. The third floor and the floor above the garages and stabling contain servants' and other rooms.

The principal façade of the Embassy, some 58 metres (189 ft) long and 17·5 metres (55 ft) high, is dominated by a giant order of engaged columns of reddish-grey Finnish granite framed at either end by pilasters. As Hoeber says, it gives no idea of the complicated economy of the interior. The columns, which have a vestigial Doric echinus and an emphatic flat abacus by way of capitals, support a cornice and a stepped parapet that hides the roof, which is a single pitched slope from front to back away from the façade. There is, consequently, a strictly horizontal silhouette to the whole façade. The side wing has giant flat pilasters. Between the columns of the façade (which is reminiscent of that of the *Kleinmotorenfabrik*) the windows are deeply set back, and have enormously exaggerated keystones and voussoirs over them, so deep that they and the sills of the window above together make up virtually the whole depth of each floor level. The architraves of the windows are also violently rusticated, so that the wall plane of the windows looks as though constructed of cyclopean masonry in contrast to the smooth ashlar (which has, however, very pronounced joints) that builds up the columns: the relationship between the vertical emphasis of the elongated columns and the horizontal emphasis of the rows of rugged voussoirs, keystones and sills was clearly intended to be one of contrast and tension, but the result is unhappy. The façade is a harsh and stiff, bombastic affair, in which two powerful forces neutralize each other.

Over the three central doors protrude three balconies, and over the centre of the cornice, on a plinth, stood a monumental pair of horse-tamers or *dioscuri* unfortunately as stiff and crude as the façade, by the Berlin sculptor (a pupil of Louis Tuaillon) Eberhard Encke.

The gatehouse of the courtyard has an attractive gable of a pattern Behrens had used before—a segmental curve with six prominent facets. This variation on the *Turbinenhalle* gable had been a keynote of the entrance and pavilion for the cement industry exhibition in Trepow the previous year.

Throughout the design of this important building, Behrens drew on a wide range of sources for inspiration when making provision for the special functions of an embassy; some of them were novel in his artistic career. Among the most obvious are derivations from Renaissance, Baroque and Mannerist palaces. The Embassy is intended to have the presence of a great Roman *palazzo* such as the Cancelleria or the Farnese, while the fretful keystones, architraves and rusticated wall surfaces which run as a secondary theme behind giant, smooth Doric columns immediately recall the Palazzo del Te. Hoeber thought that the front was a paraphrase of the Brandenburger Tor, whilst the courtyard reminded him of the 'most beautiful German Baroque courtyards; of Andreas Schlüter's grandly arranged court in the Royal Palace of Berlin'. He also thought that the Doric, marble floored entrance hall was strongly influenced by Schinkel's interior design for the *Schloss Orianda in der Krim*, and those of the Altes Museum. The façade is also an echo of the Altes Museum. The principal reception room adjacent to, and an extension of, the throne room has a richly gilded coffered ceiling reminiscent of a Venetian palace.

The principal painted decorations were by Dr Hans Wagner, an artist then based in Rome, and much of the interior decoration and furniture was designed by or in collaboration with Carl Fieger who joined Behrens' office in 1911.

The creative role, if any, played by Mies is not certain, but he said much later, 'Under Behrens I learned the grand form, if you see what I mean'. He too mentioned the Brandenburger Tor as a source of inspiration for the Embassy—'something which conveys Berlin'. Disagreements over the conduct of the building programme evidently led to Mies leaving Behrens' office soon after the contractor completed the structure in the spring of 1912.

Stanford Anderson, reporting a conversation with Mies in 1961, wrote that 'Mies's success in bringing the bids into line, after Behrens failed, made Behrens angry'; furthermore, a misunderstanding arose over details of the plans for the interior decoration which were apparently leaked to the press by accident by Mies, again annoying Behrens.[23] During another interview, Mies also recalled an exchange with Behrens about Berlage's *Beurs* (Stock Exchange), for which Behrens had earlier had great enthusiasm. It reveals once more that Behrens could easily be provoked to anger with his assistants. Mies had recently visited the *Beurs* when working in Holland on the Kröller project, and mentioned it to Behrens, who said that he was now of the opinion that the building was all *passé*'. Mies replied insubordinately 'Well, if you aren't badly mistaken', at which Behrens 'was furious; he looked as if he wanted to hit me'.[24]

The impression remains, however, that Mies was closer to Behrens emotionally and artistically than were Gropius or Jeanneret. Whilst aspects of Behrens' approach to theory and design can be recognized in the subsequent architectural careers of all three, only Mies remained faithful to Neo-Classicism and dedicated to the use of the most costly materials. His luxurious villas for rich clients are in the line of those of Behrens. When Mies was in charge of the *Weissenhof Siedlung* project for the Werkbund in 1927, Behrens was invited to participate even though (along with Hans Poelzig) he was much older than all the other architects taking part. Behrens was, it appears, generous in his turn to Mies long after they parted company; he is reported as praising the Barcelona Pavilion of 1929 as 'the most significant work of the twentieth century'.

The Embassy was of course widely discussed, and, as a State commission, represents a high point in Behrens' professional if not artistic career. Hoeber was later to claim that French and Russian protests against the 'Teutonic' façade of the Embassy were evidence of fear on the part of the *Entente* powers that their status as dictators of taste was threatened.[25] It has been considered to be something of a prototype for official architecture during the Third Reich. Hitler is known to have liked it. It attracted the admiration of an obscure architectural student in Moscow, Alfred Rosenberg, who later wrote to Behrens from his home town of Reval in Estonia, asking for advice over his career. To his surprise, Rosenberg reported, he received a courteous letter inviting him to submit some of his drawings. In the event, as Rosenberg's drawings had been left in Moscow, he did not visit Behrens in Berlin as he had planned, but travelled to Munich instead, where he met Adolf Hitler and became one of the first Nazis.[26] In the 1930s, at one point, Rosenberg became a dangerous adversary of Behrens.

The German Embassy was sacked by a Russian mob only two years after its completion, at the outbreak of the First World War. However, it is still standing today.

Notes

1. Illustrated in K. H. Hüter, *Henry van de Velde* Berlin, Akademie Verlag, 1967, ill 146, p123.
2. Herta Hesse-Frielinghaus (Ed.), *Karl Ernst Osthaus, Leben und Werk*, Reckling-hausen, Bongers, 1971, p395.
3. This plan was reproduced in Hugo Licht (Ed.), *Die Architektur des XX Jahrhunderts: Zeitschrift für moderne Baukunst* Yr. II, No. 4, 1911, pp39–40. Professor Licht obviously got hold of the earlier plan and went ahead with his publication, unaware of the changes made.
4. The Perls House, Berlin-Zehlendorf, 1911 by Mies van der Rohe has been compared with the Schroeder house, by Philip Johnson and others.
5. Fritz Hoeber, *Peter Behrens* op. cit., p89.
6. Alfred Lichtwark, *Briefe an die Kommission für die Verwaltung der Kunsthalle* (ed. by G. Pauli), Hamburg, Westermann 1923, p329.
7. Karl Ernst Osthaus, letter of 4 February 1910 to Peter Behrens. Osthaus Archiv, P 89/51.
8. Karl Ernst Osthaus to Peter Behrens, 23 December 1910. Osthaus Archiv, Kü 422/219.
9. Karl Ernst Osthaus to Peter Behrens, 16 October 1913. Osthaus Archiv, Kü 430/376.
10. Karl Ernst Osthaus to Peter Behrens, 15 September 1910. Osthaus Archiv, Kü 421/199.
11. Letter from Gropius to Helmut Weber, 5 June 1958, quoted in Weber, *Faguswerk* op. cit., p23.
12. Letter from Gropius to Osthaus, 6 March 1910. Osthaus Archiv, p89.
13. See Herta Hesse-Frielinghaus, *Briefwechsel Le Corbusier—Karl Ernst Osthaus*, Hagen, Karl Ernst Osthaus Museum, 1977. Letter 'C.I.' of 27 March 1912.
14. Nikolaus Pevsner, 'Gropius at Twenty-Six', *The Architectural Review*, Vol. 130, July 1961, pp49–51. Pevsner calls the memorandum 'one of his first attempts at creating work for himself'.
15. In the letter to Dr Herta Hesse-Frielinghaus shortly before he died, (8 May 1969, quoted on p459 of *Karl Ernst Osthaus, Leben und Werk*, op. cit.). There is a further discussion of this in Peter Stressig, 'Hohenhagen-Experimentierfeld modernen Bauens', *KEO, Leben und Werk*, op. cit., pp385–489.
16. Important studies of the Hohenhagen estate include Osthaus's own 'Die Gartenvorstadt an der Donnerkuhle', *Jahrbuch des Deutschen Werkbundes, 1912*, Jena 1912, and, more recently, Peter Stressig's work cited above (note 15); Nic Tummers' invaluable *Der Hagener Impuls*, Hagen, Linnepe, 1972, and Françoise Véry, 'J. L. M. Lauweriks: Architecte et Théosophe', *Architecture, Mouvement, Continuité*, No. 40, Sept 1976, pp55–8.
17. A commemorative album on the house was published: Johannes Geller, *Festschrift zur Einweihung des Katholischen Gesellenhauses zu Neuss. Gesellschaft für Buchdruckerei*, Neuss, 20 November 1910.
18. For a complete description of this house, its restoration and its present condition and contents, along with discussions of Behrens' Neo-Classicism, see Hoepfner,

W., and Neumeyer, F., *Das Haus Wiegand von Peter Behrens in Berlin-Dahlem*, Mainz, Phillipp von Zabern, 1979.

19. E. Schüler, *'Peter Behrens'*, *Die Kunst im Deutschen Reich, Ausgabe B: Die Baukunst*, IV, April 1940, pp6–70.

20. The house numbered XXXIII for example, in Wiegand, T., and Schrader, H. *Priene* Berlin, 1904, or Fig 124 in D. S. Robertson, *A Handbook of Greek and Roman Architecture* (2nd ed.) Cambridge, 1964, p299.

21. Peter Behrens in *Volkswirtschaftliche Blätter*, Yr. IX, No. 15, 27 August 1910, pp265–6, following a letter from Muthesius.

22. Petrov, A. N., and others, *Pamiatniki Arkhitektury Leningrada*, Leningrad, 1958.

23. Stanford Anderson, *Peter Behrens* etc. op. cit.; interview with Mies of 27 June 1961, quoted p405, n47.

24. *Mies Speaks* (Extracts from an interview given to RIAS Berlin early in 1966), *The Architectural Review* No. 862, vol cxliv, December 1968, pp451–2. The oft-quoted aphorism attributed to Mies, *'Wenig ist mehr'* ('less is more') was one of Behrens' sayings. See Werner Blaser, *'Mies van der Rohe: Lehre und Schule'*, *Exploration 3*, Basel, Birkhaüser, 1979, p89.

25. Fritz Hoeber, *Architekturfragen, Die Neue Rundschau*, 1918. See Joan Campbell, *Werkbund*, p98, n58.

26. Alfred Rosenberg, *Letzte Aufzeichnung*, Göttingen, Plesse Verlag, 1955.

8 Industrial, Commercial and Exhibition Buildings, 1911–19

Offices

In January 1911 Behrens began to work on the design of a new head office for the *Mannesmannröhren-Werke* (Mannesmann Tubes) of Düsseldorf. This well-known firm, still in existence, was at that time associated with the AEG and had Walther Rathenau on the board of Directors.

The Mannesmann office building is a five-storey rectangular block on the embankment of the Rhine in the business centre of Düsseldorf. The offices are grouped around two inner courtyards, between which a service block containing the main staircase, corridors and toilets forms a link across the middle of the building.

Behrens made a speech at the opening ceremony (10 December 1912) in which he described the design process by which he had arrived at the solution to the problems posed by this, his first office building. It was designed, interestingly enough, in the most logical way; from the office desk upwards.

The smallest room required was one to contain only one desk, at which six persons could work. This is, in a way, the unit of the building, the single cell of the whole body. Exact measurements were made of the surface of the desk, of the depth of the chair and of the room required to permit one to pass between the chair and the wall. The distance from the windows and the radiators beneath them was determined, as well as the space required for the typewriter tables and the tables for letters and documents. In addition, it was found what space was required for an unobstructed passage from door to door and for filing cases. The total gave a minimum but adequate floor area for a normal office room. The walls of this room also established at the same time the method of construction, which resulted in an arrangement of piers, in which four are at the narrow sides of the room, and also at equal intervals on the outer wall of the corridor.[1]

Nevertheless, Behrens explained, whenever he discussed the planning of the floors for different departments with his clients, he came upon an apparently insoluble problem: each Departmental Head not only wanted something different to the others, but also wanted to be able to change the layout as time and circumstances changed.

Mannesmann-Röhrenwerke, Düsseldorf, 1911–12: Head Office.

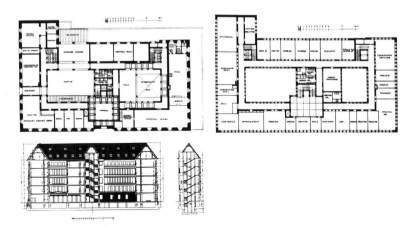

Mannesmann Head Office: Ground plan (above left); Second floor (above right), and Cross section. The drawings are to different scales.

As often as I endeavoured, in consultation with the Directors, to lay out the separate departments in the building, to assign each office of these departments to its most suitable location, just so often it became apparent that according to whether the momentary condition of business or the future development was considered, a different layout offered still greater advantages. Thus it seemed to me as if the right arrangement for definitely final purposes could never be found. In a talk with the general director of the firm it also became obvious that no solution could be found along these lines. Then I said to him: 'Even after your administrative building has been erected you will still always be in doubt as to how you are to lay out your departments to fit in with the business conditions at any specified time. Therefore I shall build you a building which is arranged like a big hall in which you can partition off rooms as you like to meet the requirements that may arise at any moment . . .' For this reason supporting cross walls were not employed in the construction, the whole building being erected on a system of open floors. The walls that now partition off the various large or small rooms are free, soundproof partitions which can be taken out without much trouble or set up in other places . . . The plan shows how all the offices lie on the outside of the building and are without exception lighted by the same arrangement of windows . . . For that reason, this building is at present writing one of the brightest and best lighted office buildings in existence.

He also claimed that the provision of three windows per office unit, situated between the four piers, gave a bright, shadowless but diffuse light in the room, rather than a single harsh source of light.

The Mannesmann building is a steel-framed construction clad in stone. The base is sharply battered, in rusticated limestone, and the upper storeys are in smooth ashlar; the roof is steeply sloping, and clad in slate. That the finished ensemble was like a Florentine *palazzo* was not only obvious to contemporaries, but was mentioned by Behrens himself in his address, in which he cited the Palazzo Strozzi and the Medici-Riccardi as prototypes for the monumental, compact, closed form he wished to achieve. (The building also superficially resembles Alfred Messel's 1905 AEG Head Office building on the Friedrich-Karl Ufer in Berlin. Behrens expressed his long admiration for Messel in the obituary he wrote in 1909, in which he specifically mentioned the AEG building and, in connection with it, Messel's Palladianism.)

The entrance, on the river front, had Doric columns on either side of the door, and originally a relief sculpture by Eberhard Encke in the tympanum.[2] The building was extended (not by Behrens) in the 1930s, and is still in excellent condition.[3]

Another, related, office building was the administrative headquarters (1911/12–20) for the Continental-Caoutchouc-und Guttapercha Kompanie (Continental Rubber Company) in Hannover-Vahrenwald. The structure and office planning system was almost identical to that of the Mannesmann, although the Hannover building (destroyed during the Second World War) was larger, with a façade of about 100 metres (328 ft) in length and a strongly horizontal roof line above four storeys on a low rusticated base. The corner pilasters are like those of the Altes Museum. The office accommodation is around two courtyards which are on either side of a large central hall. This is arcaded and pillared like the *cortile* of a Florentine palace.

Begun in 1912, it was only just completed by 1914, and used as a military warehouse during the war. It was restored and completed by 1920.

Continental Caoutchouc-und Guttapercha-werk, Hannover, 1911–12: Hall.

A building of not dissimilar appearance was designed for the AEG as a new head office on the Humbolthain in 1917, but was never carried out. Yet another related project appears to have been the offices of the T-Z Gitter-werke in Berlin-Tempelhof (1911–12).

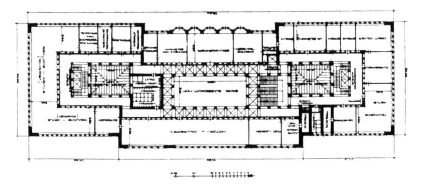

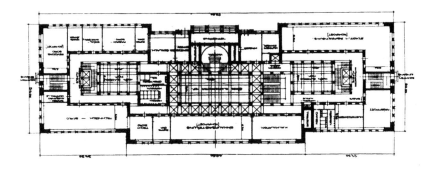

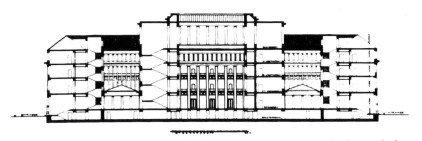

Continental Rubber Company Head Office: Upper floor plan (top); Ground plan (middle), and Cross section (bottom).

Architecture for industry and public services

Among the most remarkable project drawings to come from the office of Peter Behrens were those related to an AEG-sponsored electric railway line that was planned to run from Gesundbrunnen in the north of Berlin (close by the Humbolthain) to Neukölln in the south. This was the subject of AEG plans between 1907 and 1914, but was never carried out. Sections of this proposed line were obliged to run as an overhead railway, although the greater part was to have been underground. Between 1910 and 1912 Behrens

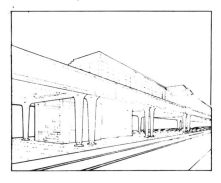

Overhead Railway station: Perspective, c 1910.

prepared drawings of a steel viaduct raised on single stanchions in line, and two versions of an elevated railway station, perhaps intended for Gesundbrunnen.[4] Sabine Bohle sees Behrens' hand in the design of a projected underground station at Neanderstrasse of 1915, and Behrens is also credited with the design of the U-Bahn Moritzplatz, although there is nothing remaining today above or below ground that can be attributed to Behrens.[5] It was a short step for Behrens from designing railway stations, to designing a diesel electric passenger locomotive for the AEG. An example of this interesting design was found in reasonable condition as recently as 1964.

A suspension bridge over the Rhine

At the beginning of 1911, Behrens took part (along with Max Berg, Hans Poelzig and others) in the competition to design a new bridge over the Rhine between Cologne and Deutz. His design, prepared in collaboration with the Dortmund 'Union' steel construction company, was for a suspension bridge with the carriageway slung from two pylons standing on caissons in the river. For the approach to the bridge on either side of the river, Behrens planned groups of buildings along the lines of the Mannesmann head office, but raised on rusticated arcading, forming an embankment rather like the Adam brothers' 'Adelphi' scheme in London. His submission was not, however, successful.

Design for a bridge over the Rhine, Cologne, 1910–11.

The Frankfurt Gasanstalt

A major industrial complex which was, however, built and which still stands, was the Gasworks at the then new East Harbour of Frankfurt-am-Main. As with the AEG factories in Berlin, the various buildings are disposed around a railway branch line. The furnaces (retort houses) at the western end, are between stockpiles of coal on the one hand and those of the by-product of the process, coke, on the other. The gasholders are at the far (eastern) end of the site, as far away as possible. Between these two groups lies a remarkable range of carefully related buildings designed by Behrens: on the south side the processing plant, and on the north those for the administration, for the technicians and the workforce.

The rectangular buildings consist of an L-shaped power house containing electrical generators; a steam boiler, a laboratory and the purifying plant; a plant for the treatment of ammonia by-products, and a large apparatus building. These are all in the best tradition of small-scale nineteenth-century industrial buildings, and they are well-proportioned, low, and with Schinkelesque low-pitched or mansard roofs. The meticulous detailing of the brickwork is striking; the tall rectangular windows are recessed in broad shallow architraves between the piers. The classicism here is to be found in the proportion, and in restrained details like dentilled cornices.

It is between these buildings that the most spectacular structure was situated: a tall cylindrical water tower connected to three lower cylindrical towers, each joined to its neighbour by an arched bridge.[6] These three towers (in violet-brown glazed brick) contained pumps and vessels for the storage and processing of tar and ammonia liquor—both industrially valuable by-products of the manufacture of gas. These powerfully shaped exercises in basic solid geometry have been either described as Expressionist architecture before its time, or seen in terms of Ledoux's Neo-Classical industrial complex at Arc-et-Senans. The cross-section of the group reveals,

Frankfurter Gasgesellschaft, 1911–12: Perspective.

133

Frankfurter Gasgesellschaft: Former offices, 1911–12.

Frankfurter Gasgesellschaft: Water tower, 1911–12.

however, that there was little room for fantasy, formalism or expressionism: there is no part of the structure that is not close in its dimensions to the minimum required by function. This function, that of submitting solids, liquids and gases to chemical processes, inevitably imposed highly individual forms on the component parts of this industrial plant and on the physical relationship of these parts. Their disposition was determined, as was their form, to a high degree by physics, not by human scale or activity. Aesthetic control, therefore, was reduced to within very narrow limits (as with so many of the electrical appliances that Behrens styled): the resolution of untidy details into neat, smooth forms; the control of proportions where permissible, and the application of close attention to surface colour and texture. (The towers have, nevertheless, an amusing coincidental resemblance to the Eschenheimer Turm in Frankfurt).

On the north border of the site are ranged the workshops, the welfare building, the offices, a house for the factory manager, and a gatehouse. A building for meters and regulators, a little further inside the site, completes the composition. For all the banality of the industry to which these buildings are dedicated, they are, nevertheless, a surprise: beautifully studied in their formal relationship to one another, as well as carefully proportioned and detailed in themselves. The manager's house was as seriously treated as one of the Eppenhausen villas, artistically speaking, and the gatehouse has a relationship to this house similar to that of the garden pergola to the Wiegand house. Along Schielestrasse, these buildings are strung out and coded in their colour in such a way as to gradually draw a distinction between the domestic and industrial use of each one. Thus the manager's house is of yellow brick with dark brown accents, such as the capitals of the square piers; the office building uses yellow and dark brown clinker bricks in a more equal proportion; the proportion of yellow brick used in the welfare building is less, whilst the workshop and the other buildings are all of dark brown brick.

Behrens had come a long way from the days of his *Feste des Lebens und der Kunst*: from dreams of building a fantastic temple of the beautiful drama of life, to designing hard, tight factory buildings for a gasworks on an industrial wasteland. While he may still have believed the theatre to be the highest symbol of a culture, he was now clearly accepting all manifestations of modern culture to be the subject of serious consideration by the artist.

Exhibitions, 1910–1914
Behrens made important contributions to two exhibitions in 1910: the Cement Industry Exhibition in Berlin-Treptow, and the World's Fair in Brussels. Both these exhibitions took place in the summer.

The Brussels Exhibition
Behrens was responsible for major parts of the German section: the Machine Hall, the Railway Hall, the Hall of the Union of German Engineers, the

Machine Hall, Brussels Exhibition, 1910.

exhibition room of the *Delmenhorster Linoleumfabrik* and the Press room and library of the Union of Illustrated Magazine Publishers. The *Werkbund* helped to organize the German contribution to the Fair.

The Machine Hall was a graceful variant of the *Turbinenhalle* and the *Montagehalle* of the AEG. As it was not a real factory, however, greater liberties could be taken with its form, notably in the height to which it rose internally above the travelling crane that ran, in a similar fashion to those of the AEG factories, along the axis of the building.

It consisted of a broad central nave 23 metres (74 ft) wide and of about the same height, with two side aisles each 7 metres (22 ft) wide. Eight bays long, it measured about 35 metres (114 ft). The main vertical steel stanchions of the nave supported arched girders that were cantilevered steeply up on one side to form the main roof of the hall, and steeply down on the other side to form the roof of the side aisles. Joined to these girders were arches spanning the central void and, on the perimeter of the structure, lesser vertical stanchions supported the edge of the aisle roof. These acted also as an anchorage for the extreme cantilever of the central void.

The inner curved profiles of these arches were handsome. They were painted dark blue, while the inner surface of the roof was clad in white tongue-and-groove boarding. Only the central area was glazed, which emphasized the balance and poise of the structure. It displayed heavy machinery and motors by different manufacturers.

Theodor Heuss (one of the strongest early supporters of the *Werkbund*, who later became famous as Germany's first *Bundespräsident* after the Second World War), wrote with enthusiasm in *Die Hilfe* in June 1910 about Behrens' new hall:

Where pure steel construction triumphantly progresses, at the same time, artistic awareness has developed, and a man has been found who endows it with a slim and firm monumentality; who has a strong inward sensitivity for all the economy of engineering. That is Peter Behrens.

Monumentality was, incidentally, a favourite word in Behrens' circle. One can sympathize with the typist who, in 1909, accidentally put that 'Herr Professor Behrens has monumentally gone on a fourteen-day journey' in a letter to Osthaus from the office. He corrected it by substituting *momentanlich* (for the moment).[7]

The Hall of the Union of German Engineers contained material in showcases and on screens, and so was not designed to resemble a factory. It was constructed, like the Railways Hall, largely out of wood, and had two-storey galleries on either side of the central space. Above these, from heavy, rounded consoles set against a sort of frieze of metopes, were suspended tent-like draperies. The hall for displaying railway engines was constructed (in collaboration with the Munich engineer Hermann Kügler) of laminated wooden beams, according to a patent process, the *System Hetzerinl-Formen*. As the *Maschinenhalle* resembled a model factory, so this hall was designed to suggest a railway station.

The Cement Industry Exhibition
This was an exhibition of building materials including lime, plaster, clay, artificial stone, cement and reinforced concrete. It was organized in conjunction with the third Annual General Meeting of the *Werkbund*, and was aimed at persuading engineers, architects and industrialists to exploit the artistic and practical potential of synthetic materials.[8]

Behrens created two adjacent rectangular courtyards in front of the pavilions for the cement and lime industries, both with sunken gardens in the middle. The cement industry pavilion and the gateway were both given gables curving in six facets. A small two-storey house was also constructed. These buildings and courtyards contained features demonstrating the uses and properties of the various products, and included artificial stone figures by Richard Engelmann of Dahlem.

The World's Fair, Ghent
In the summer of 1913, a room was devoted to Peter Behrens' work as a retrospective exhibition; this was arranged by the *Deutsches Museum für Kunst in Handel und Gewerbe* (The German Museum of Commercial and

Ton, Zement und Kalk Industrie Ausstellung, Berlin, 1910.

Festival Hall, Werkbund Exhibition, Cologne, 1914.

Applied Art), an organization set up by Behrens' patron Osthaus. Osthaus thought the room to be the focal point of the exhibition, and was able to tell Behrens that he was to receive the Grand Prix for it. Under the same auspices, a travelling exhibition of German industrial art and of craft work had been sent to the United States the year before; this exhibition contained much work by Behrens, and he designed the catalogue. These two exhibitions contributed to his reputation at home and abroad.[9] The climax of this reputation perhaps came with the publication of the handsome and substantial monograph on Behrens by Fritz Hoeber in 1913—a unique distinction for a living German architect at that time, and unusual for an architect of any nationality other than Wright and Lutyens. In the same year, Behrens was elected to the Executive Committee of the *Werkbund*, and as such was a committee member responsible for the 1914 *Werkbund* exhibition in Cologne.

The Werkbund Exhibition, 1914
This was to be the largest and most comprehensive *Werkbund* exhibition hitherto, and included craftwork, industrial design, graphic design, architecture and town planning. Osthaus asked Behrens to help him with the design of the room for exhibiting 'Masterworks of Applied Art' at this exhibition. More importantly, however, Behrens also designed the central *Festhalle* of the exhibition, a hall that would serve for lectures, debates and the seventh Annual General Meeting of the organization.

A long rectangular hall, its façade was a variation on the theme of Alberti's S. Andrea, Mantua, having a fusion of the temple front and triumphal arch motifs. Within the arch above the entrance, Behrens placed a cast of Encke's *Dioscuri* from the St Petersburg Embassy. The interior was not unlike that of the Hagen crematorium.

This interior was the scene of the celebrated debate on the future direction of the *Werkbund* that took place between Hermann Muthesius and Henry van der Velde and their supporters. This bitter and explosive argument has been described and discussed in some detail in recent years.[10]

Briefly, the affair was as follows: Muthesius, in his opening Address (which he had anticipated with a printed summary of ten basic principles—'*Leitsätze*'—as a proposal for the *Werkbund*'s future activity) stressed industrial and economic issues as being of supreme importance, and that the role of the designer should be one of developing and refining standardized functional units, canons or types for use in architecture and the applied arts. This he called '*Typisierung*'. He was bitterly opposed by Van de Velde, who, as an artist, regarded artistic freedom as inviolate, and the role of the *Werkbund*, broadly speaking, as that of an organization to raise the standard of public taste and the quality of the environment. Gropius, who later characterized himself as the enfant terrible of the affair, and who disliked Muthesius intensely for various reasons, saw in this dispute a chance of attacking his authority, and of perhaps thrusting himself, Gropius, into a position of leadership within the *Werkbund*. To that end he whipped up the opposition, and conspired with Osthaus to threaten a secession from the *Werkbund* of all Muthesius's opponents.

In all this, Behrens, although inclining more towards the standpoint of Van de Velde, acted as a moderating influence.

I must say openly that I am not altogether clear what Herr Muthesius meant by '*Typisierung*'. I have, moreover, come to think that a rigid canon should not be understood by it. I have thought of archetypes in art as, for me, the highest aim of any artistic activity. It is the strongest and ultimate impression of a profound personality. It is the conception of an object in its most mature and clear distillation, a solution free from all secondary considerations. The best work of an artist, from both these factors, will always constitute 'types'. It is self-evident that, for example, a department store that stands out as a significant expression of such a thing is better architecture than if it takes on the appearance of a castle.

In earlier times, the constant striving for perfection led to, for example, the point where the ground plan of a house could not be better designed than by ensuring that all its aesthetic and functional needs were served. The result was a typical, standardized town house, that was repeated with slight variations. It is in this sense that I understand 'archetypal' art. Artistic freedom shouldn't come into it. But the guarantee of artistic freedom must be one of the sacred precepts of the *Werkbund*'s endeavour. . . .'

He further said that art ought not to be considered as one's private affair, as a mistress to be served; that we no longer want an aesthetic that takes its standards from romantic daydreams, but one based on the realities of life. Professor August Hoff recalled hearing Behrens speaking during the debate, which he had attended when a young student; he had been taken there by the painter Thorn Prikker. He remembered Behrens' voice as 'manly and sonorous'. Hoff also remembered Behrens' as reserved, and with a patrician pride, although, in an intimate circle, pleasant and humorous.[11]

While away from the conference, in Darmstadt, Behrens sent a telegram to Osthaus:

Hear from Berlin over conflict through articles in newspapers. Certainly for unconditional freedom of individual creativity, but hold it as necessary that *Werkbund* should be preserved on this basis. Advise above all avoid secession and bring about clarification through pronouncements by authoritative persons, in which case dissention would be foolish and to be regretted. Believe me to be your friend in this affair. Behrens.[12]

Osthaus and Gropius were annoyed to find that Behrens advised moderation. 'Vague in his attitudes as ever', Osthaus wrote to Gropius, 'Behrens' position is very doubtful. It appears that he wants to play the role of the great mediator'.[13] Subsequent relations between Osthaus and Behrens are reported to have been distant.

Very shortly, the controversy was shelved. Although Behrens' poster for the exhibition gave its planned duration as May to October, it had only just opened in July; in August war broke out. The exhibition closed, and within a few weeks the halls and pavilions were temporary hospitals, full of wounded soldiers from the Western Front.

An unexecuted project
Early in 1913, Behrens was involved in the projected redesigning of the Holstentorplatz in Lübeck, a matter which had concerned the people of that town for many years, involving reports, proposals and competitions.[14] A memorial to the Kaiser Wilhelm I was decided upon, in the form of a *Volkshaus*, which would be a public centre with a library and lecture theatre; the siting of an equestrian statue of Wilhelm by Louis Tuaillon, a new bridge over the Trave, and the creation of a square as a setting for the whole, incorporating the medieval Holstentor with its fat round towers. Behrens prepared several Neo-Classical schemes. His competition entry was for a very plain rectangular block with closely spaced tall windows running the entire length of the upper floor, and a triangular pedimented entrance portico. This central block had pavilions on either side, embracing a wide space. Another earlier design had a very Palladian character, with a prominent central dome. The limited competition was won with a Gothic revival design by Emil Blunck. A controversy regarding the relative 'modernity' and 'eclecticism' of Behrens' and the winning design ran for some time in the *Lübeckischer Blätter* and elsewhere, only perhaps memorable for the ardent support for Behrens' design given by Arthur Moeller van den Bruck. Moeller van den Bruck, who was later to gain notoriety as author of *Das Dritte Reich* (1922), a book considered as formative for literate adherents of National Socialism, praised Behrens as architectural heir to the tradition of Schinkel and Gilly in his *Der Preussische Stil* (1916); which, although fundamentally conservative and patriotic, was another cult book among what passed for intellectuals among the Nazis. This praise went some way, in later years, to rehabilitate Behrens (and Hans Poelzig, Behrens' predecessor as Professor at the Prussian Academy of Arts, who was also singled out for commendation by Moeller) in the eyes of some of the authorities during the Third Reich.

C. W. Julius Blancke-Werke
Behrens' first contact with the firm of C. W. Julius Blancke-Werke (of Merseburg an der Saale) was to design dials for pressure-gauges of their manufacture. In January 1912, however, he was invited to design a new factory building to be set in an estate of houses for the employees. A range of different types of accommodation was designed, from rooms for unmarried employees to detached houses for engineers, clerical workers and so on. The main estate was to have been of two-storey terraced housing and four-storey blocks for the families of manual workers. With steep roofs and dormer windows, the general appearance of the housing was cottage-like, and the setting allowed for gardens, trees and a generous park. As at

Hennigsdorf, the rows of workers' houses were mostly in a continuous line, but this line broke alternatively forwards and back at right angles to the streets, to give garden forecourts and variation to the setting.

A variant of the garden suburb idea, the drawings show the houses to be pleasantly set amongst thickly planted trees. As early as 1908, Behrens had stated his preference for compact groups of houses rather than the dispersed scattering of the kind suggested by Ebenezer Howard.[15] Hoeber, at the time these designs were being made, mentioned Voysey as a possible influence, along with historical German examples of simple housing, like the *Fuggerei* in Augsburg or the *Grabenhäuschen* in Ulm—sixteenth and seventeenth century survivals.

The War Years

Behrens' contract with the AEG was terminated in 1914. Although it was not formally renewed, he continued to work on AEG projects from time to time—the NAG factory at Oberschöneweide for example, and the factories at Hennigsdorf. His assistant Jean Krämer took a similar post as architectural consultant to the AEG in his place.

Responding to the wave of patriotic feeling that swept the country, Behrens was a signatory to the notorious Manifesto of German University Professors and Men of Science (the 93 German Intellectuals). This, addressed *An die Kulturwelt*, defended Germany against the charge of having been guilty of causing the outbreak of war, and against censure for having invaded neutral Belgium. Other notable signatories were Dehmel, Klinger, Liebermann, Reinhardt, Planck, von Stuck, Trübner and Wiegand. Behrens helped to found the *Bund deutscher Gelehrter und Künstler* (League of German Artists and Men of Learning) which identified some 1,000 politically unaffiliated intellectuals and artists with the German cause, which was broadly speaking seen by them as a struggle against British Imperialism; a battle for national and cultural survival. They advocated a negotiated peace without annexation of territory on either side, and the artistic membership tended to disassociate itself from the connection (encouraged by many—Friedrich Naumann, for example) between the aspirations of the *Werkbund* on the one hand and German foreign policy on the other, that is to say an overt support for a policy of industrial and cultural domination in Europe through expansion and the export trade.[16]

Nevertheless, although too old at forty-six to be a combatant, Behrens obtained permission personally from the Kaiser to wear his uniform (he had been made an officer during his reserve military service in the 1890s)[17] and several times visited the IX Army corps on the Eastern Front with General Scheffer. He also took part in the limited competition for a *Haus der Freundschaft* (House of Friendship) for the German-Turkish Union in Constantinople. This idea, felt by some to be an imperialist venture, was promoted by Ernst Jäckh (then the *Werkbund*'s executive secretary) and was to provide a library and reading room, a concert hall, theatre, exhibition space, café and so on, to encourage the consolidation of German-Turkish friendship. The Turks donated the site, the German-Turkish Union provided funds, and the patronage of the Kaiser and the Sultan was obtained. In 1916, twelve architects were invited to submit designs, although one of them, Gropius, was unable to compete as he could not obtain leave from the army.[18] Behrens' entry was second to that of German Bestelmeyer. The scheme was only partly built.

During the war, efforts were made on both sides in the conflict to influence neutral countries with cultural events of various kinds; to this end the *Werkbund* organized exhibitions at the *Gewerbemuseum* in Basel (March–April), the Winterthur Museum (May–June); in Berne (July) and in Copenhagen, during the year 1917–18. The Foreign Office subsidized these exhibitions. Behrens was responsible for the Swiss exhibitions and designed a very attractive, demountable, prefabricated wooden pavilion for the one in Berne. Gustav Ammann, a Swiss gardener who worked with Behrens on the garden for this pavilion, remembered him with pleasure in a note prompted by the news of his death in 1940:

By any standards Peter Behrens was an amiable person. He had a special inclination for plants. He often appeared, on his travels, at the Froebel nursery gardens and wanted to see the latest Christmas roses. On his property in Babelsberg, he tenderly nursed his garden as a true enthusiast.[19]

At this time, Behrens and Muthesius, as *Werkbund* representatives, were advising the government on architectural and building matters, on the *Normenausschuss der deutschen Industrie* (The Committee for German Industrial Standards). Subsequently, the *DIN-Format* (*Deutsche Industrie-Normen*, German Industrial Standard) began to be applied to a wide range of industrial products.

An interesting war-time undertaking was the finely proportioned factory (1917) and aircraft hangars (1919) for the *Hannover'sche Waggonfabrik AG* (Linden). The interior of the factory workshop is not unlike the Brussels *Machinenhalle*.

A good deal of the work of Behrens' office during the war was, however, directed towards low-cost housing: an estate at Lichtenberg (an eastern suburb of Berlin) of which only a small part was realized, 1915–18; an estate at Spandau (to the west of Berlin), 1917; both have much in common with the Merseburg plan.

In 1918, a few houses were added to the AEG housing at Hennigsdorf. This row, on Paul Jordan-Strasse, comprises eleven semi-detached houses (twenty-two dwellings) arranged in such a way that every third building is set back from the others in the Greek meander-pattern familiar to us since the Rathenaustrasse housing of 1911. The striking thing about these simple two-storey houses with their low-pitched roofs is the novel material out of which they were built. Owing to the shortage of materials, concrete and clinker breeze-block were used, and left unrendered.

(Left) Houses at Hennigsdorf, 1918–20.

(Below) Hannover'sche Waggonfabrik, Aircraft Hangar, Hannover, 1915.

(Bottom) Werkbund Pavilion, Berne, 1917.

In the immediate post-war period, two housing schemes in eastern Germany are of great interest. One, of 1919, was for a community of industrial workers at the textile town of Forst (Lausitz) now on the border with Poland. Taking into account the pattern of life of the people, traditionally divided between work in the factories and work on their own smallholdings, the houses were closely related to market gardens and allotments, with moveable fencing between the fields so that machinery held in common could be used for ploughing. In this way, the persistence of a half-peasant, half-proletarian way of life, usually disrupted, or only carried on in the teeth of industrialization, was provided for and administered by the co-operative.

A similar scheme in Silesia at Neusalz (now Nowasól, Poland) on the Oder was remarkable for the fact that Behrens canvassed the views of the mining community concerning their future homes. He described the role of the architect, in this connection, as a co-ordinator implementing the wishes of the builders and the users (many of whom were, of course, war veterans).[20] The two outstanding requests he received were for an absence of steps or stairs within the house, and for the entrance to be through a garden that could be seen from the windows. Behrens and his colleague Heinrich de Fries developed three house types. The first, a two-storey house containing four flats with a communal staircase had a continuous balcony along the upper floor level. The gardens of the ground floor apartments lay on one side of the row, and those of the upper floors on the other. A second type had the stairs to the upper flats on one side of the house, joining the balcony directly from the gardens on that side. A third type had one-family houses in rows, with corner buildings containing four flats. These ideas, giving each unit of a fairly high-density low-cost housing scheme its own private garden, overlooked from all the living rooms, was called by Behrens the 'double

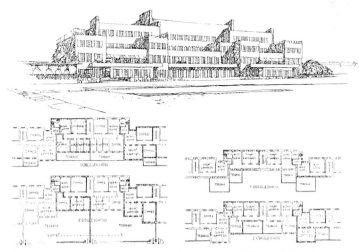

Terrassenhäuser, 1920: Perspective drawing (above); Plans (below).

145

garden house' system. They were further developed into a design he called the *Terrassenhaus*, a four-storey apartment block with each level providing a roof garden for the apartment above it. A development of this idea was built as Behrens' contribution to the *Weissenhofsiedlung* in 1927.

As a result of this intensive work on housing for the masses (other plans were made for Spandau as mentioned earlier; for Potsdam-Nowawes; for Grossenbaum and for Babelsberg in 1920), Behrens and Heinrich de Fries jointly published a booklet *Vom sparsamen Bauen* (On Economical Building) in 1918. It is a discussion of the problems of achieving speed and economy in building at a time when materials were in short supply and new housing desperately needed. They argued that a standardized layout be adopted for basic types of habitation, 'thought out from the worker's point of view'; that modern constructional methods, using reinforced concrete and breeze block, should be rationalized to allow for the most extensive possible use of machinery in the production and assembly of building materials for mass housing. A harmonious combination of rows of small houses, each with its own allotment garden, and low-rise multi-storey tenement blocks would create suburbs offering varied types of accommodation. The authors sharply criticized 'sentimentality and false romanticism' in the custom of some architects who modelled workers' housing on small-town and village traditions (a tendency of architects who later actively favoured Nazism).

Built-in cupboards and other fixed accessories would be, they suggested, cheaper than free-standing furniture; moreover smaller, lighter and cheaper furniture should be designed to make the maximum use of space. The fitting-out of ship's cabins was cited as an illustration of how such furnishings could provide an acceptably pleasant and comfortable environment. The brochure also suggests, as did Behrens' 1908 article *Die Gartenstadtbewegung* (the Garden City movement),[21] the inclusion in housing schemes of communal services such as a crèche, baths, a library, a meeting-hall and so on.

The central theme of *Vom sparsamen Bauen* is, of course, workers' housing, and as such, consciously or unconsciously the essay affirms a belief in a hierarchy of class-orientated housing. For civil servants and managerial staff of the Hamburg shipbuilding industry, Behrens could revert wholly to the Garden Suburb approach in the English sense. His estate for the *Deutsche Werft* at Altona Othmarschen (1920) is of individual brick-built houses with huge picturesque roofs of an angle of about 45°, in remarkable contrast to his other contemporary schemes.

Notes

1. This and subsequent quotations from Behrens on the Mannesmann building are from Peter Behrens: 'Administration Buildings for Industrial Plants', *American Architect* cxxviii, August 26 1925, p167ff, translated from Peter Behrens, *Zur Erinnerung an die Einweihung des Verwaltungsgebäudes der Mannesmann Röhrenwerke in Düsseldorf, 10 Dezember 1912*, Düsseldorf, Mannesmann, 1913.

2. Stanford Anderson (op. cit., p403, n35) quotes Henry Russell Hitchcock as believing that the hall and stairs were detailed by Mies van der Rohe.

3. The planning flexibility of the structure was regarded by Hoeber (and by Cremers, who was writing in 1928) as a landmark in office design.

4. Sabine Bohle, *'Peter Behrens und die Schnellbahnpläne der AEG'*, *Industriekultur* op. cit., p199ff.

5. Rave, R. and Knöfel, H.-J., *Bauen seit 1900 in Berlin*, Berlin, Kiepert, 1968, and the comments and quotations relating to the U-Bahn Moritzplatz in *Berlin und Seine Bauten, Teil X*, B. and B. Berlin, Wilhelm Ernst, 1979. There are useful references to other Behrens buildings in *Berlin und Seine Bauten*; for example *Teil IX, Industriebauten, Bürohäuser* (1971) and *Teil IV, Wohnungsbau* (1975).

6. Two towers were demolished about 1979. The whole site is threatened with redevelopment, as Frankfurt uses North Sea gas from Holland nowadays, and the plant is redundant.

7. A letter of 6 September 1909 to Osthaus, Osthaus Archiv, Kü 418/118.

8. See Joan Campbell, *Werkbund* op. cit., p50.

9. Behrens also had a retrospective exhibition at the *Kunstgewerbemuseum* in Frankfurt in February 1909, and a special room at the Exhibition of Christian Art at Düsseldorf in the same year.

10. The best discussions of this event are in Barbara Miller Lane', *Architecture and Politics in Germany 1918–1945*, Cambridge, Mass, Harvard, 1968; Marcel Franciscono, *Walter Gropius and the creation of the Bauhaus in Weimar*, Chicago, University of Illinois, 1971; Joan Campbell, *The German Werkbund*, Princeton, Princeton UP, 1978; Peter Stressig, 'Walter Gropius', *Karl Ernst Osthaus, Leben und Werk* op. cit., and in the publication of letters in the Osthaus Archive relating to the controversy, by Anna-Christa Funk, *Karl Ernst Osthaus Gegen Hermann Muthesius*, Hagen, KEO Museum, 1978. There is also much material in the Osthaus Archiv, filed under DWB/K (Ausstellung Köln).

11. Professor August Hoff, *'Peter Behrens, Persönlichkeit und Werk'*, *Aussprachen, (gehalten auf der 8 Tagung der Henry van de Velde Gesellschaft am 30.10.66)* Hagen, Henry van de Velde Gesellschaft, 1966.

12. Telegram in Osthaus Archiv, Kü 382.

13. Letter from Osthaus to Gropius, 14 July 1914. Osthaus Archiv, Kü 385/1.

14. See Stanford Anderson, op. cit., p407, n52, and Christa Pieske, *'Die Gestaltung des Holstentorplatzes in Lübeck, 1906–1913–1926'*, *Deutsche Kunst und Denkmalpflege*, Yr. 33, No. 1/2, 1975.

15. Peter Behrens, *Die Gartenstadtbewegung*, *Berliner Tageblatt*, March 5 1908.

16. See Joan Campbell, *Werkbund*, op. cit., p98.

17. Peter Behrens, *Ahnentafel*, 1933 (Family Tree and Personal History) deposited at the *Akademie der Künste*, Berlin.

18. The invited architects were Behrens, Bestelmeyer, Bonatz, Eberhardt, Elsaesser, Endell, Fischer, Gropius, Paul, Poelzig, Riemerschmid and Taut.

19. Gustav Ammann, *Nochmals Peter Behrens*, *Das Werk*, Yr. 27, October 1940, p302. There are interesting minutes of the meetings of the *Werkbund* at which the Swiss exhibition projects were discussed, in the Osthaus Archiv, Hagen; DWB 3/4.

20. Peter Behrens, *Vorstand*, June 20 1919, pp4, 6. (Joan Campbell, *Werkbund* op. cit., p126, n65.)
21. Peter Behrens, *Die Gartenstadtbewegung*, op. cit.

9 The Twenties and Thirties

Behrens welcomed the new Republic. In an article of 1919 he wrote that the new time called for a cultural expression of its spirit; every effort should be made to achieve that cultural level at which a universal art would develop under the leadership of architecture.[1] At a practical level he contributed to the framing of the Republican Constitution of the Reich at the invitation of the National Constituent Assembly in Weimar.

At the same time he withdrew from the executive of the *Werkbund* in order to take a purely advisory status. The conservative elements in the *Werkbund* were once more under pressure from the Left and the more avant-garde, as they had been in 1914. Although by this time Behrens was clearly one of the conservative 'elder statesmen' of the organization, he, like Poelzig, gave reasonable consideration to the idea of amalgamating the activist *Arbeitsrat für Kunst* (Working Council for Art) with which Gropius was closely associated. Nevertheless, Gropius characterized Behrens, along with Poelzig, Paul and Muthesius, as *'Architekten-Hochstapler'* ('architects-on-the-make'). At this stage Behrens evidently had no great hostility towards strongly republican radical organizations; he exhibited a model for a tower block on the Kemperplatz (1921) with the *Novembergruppe* in 1924. By 1925 he was apparently a member, and exhibited with them again in 1926.[2]

One thing is very striking about the immediate post-war years: Behrens temporarily threw over the *sachlichkeit* (common-sense objectivity) which, combined with Neo-Classicism, had been characteristic of 'Behrens-Stil'. He was one of those who emerged from the war years designing buildings as expressionist as the paintings of the artists associated with the *November-gruppe*. One of the earliest of such buildings was one of his major achievements: the new headquarters for Hoechst.

Hoechst *Farbwerke* (formerly Meister Lucius und Brüning) was part of the enormous IG Farben, (the initials IG stood for *Interessen-Gesellschaft*, meaning a community of interest), one of the half-dozen German companies that had emerged before the First World War to dominate world production of synthetic dyestuffs. Hoechst also had a pharmaceutical department.

During the period that Behrens worked on the new technical headquarters, administration and research building for Hoechst, Germany was

Hoechst, Head Offices for Hoechst Dyeworks, 1920–24.

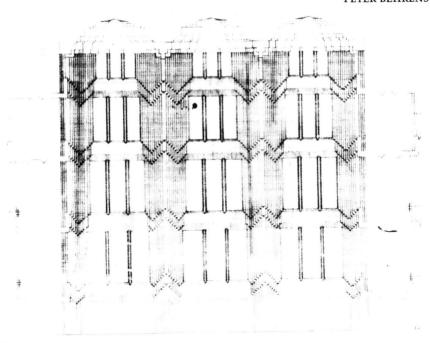

Hoechst: Cross-section of hall.

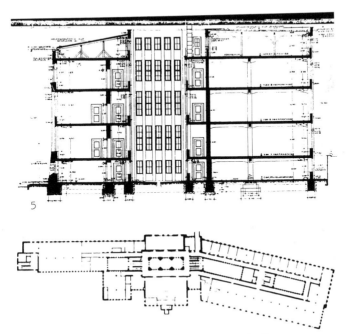

Hoechst: Plan (below), and Cross-section of offices and hall.

151

experiencing violent political and social convulsions in the immediate aftermath of the war: Frankfurt (which had been bombed during the war) was occupied by the French in 1920 after the Kapp *Putsch*; in January 1923 the French occupied the whole of the Rhine and the Ruhr, which was then paralysed by a total strike. By the summer of 1923, moreover, the Mark, which had begun to slide in 1921, had fallen in value to one million to the dollar. Behrens was obliged during the commission to write (in 1921) to ask for an additional clause to be agreed in his contract, that his Honorarium should be index-linked against inflation.[3] The economic scene was clouded by the passive resistance of factories that had ceased production, by demonstrations, arrests and shootings, and by French exploitation of chemical technology taken from the IG Farben in various ways. A permit from the French authorities had to be obtained in order to enter or leave the territory.

Behrens was invited to design the new technical headquarters in August 1920 by Geheimrat Adolf Haeuser, the then Managing Director. Haeuser, a lawyer, not a scientist, had a great interest in art and a large personal collection of pictures.

The invitation stressed the urgency of the matter, and so early the next month Behrens was ready with preliminary plans and suggestions. The brief called for administrative offices, drawing offices, laboratories, archives, a lecture theatre and an exhibition hall, on a long narrow site across the road from the existing office building. Behrens proposed a central rectangular block with the main entrance directly opposite that of the old building. The two buildings were to be linked with a bridge, springing from the base of a tower, so that, as Behrens put it, 'the combination of the two buildings, the bridge and the tower, will give picturesque approaches from the Hoechst or the Mainz directions'.

On either side of this central composition the two slightly lower office wings follow the slight obtuse angle of the road, to give a total façade of about 150 metres (492 ft) length.

The style of the building (which is still in good condition) is remarkably different from anything Behrens had done before. The tower has a large and fanciful clock face with Gothic numerals on the Mainz side, and a smaller clock on the other. The bridge has a small V-shaped oriel window in the centre on either side. The dominant theme is, however, the parabolic arch. This is used both for the great bridge and for the upper range of windows of the tower, the central block beside it and the offices. The voussoirs of these arches are dramatically radiating courses of brickwork. The whole building is executed in bricks of two contrasting textures. The bases of the wings are sharply battered, and the rectangular office windows are grouped vertically in deep recesses. The effect is not one of pillars or pilasters, however, as against this vertical emphasis horizontal bands of contrasting brick run the whole length of the façade. The arches and the expressive brickwork are reminiscent of the contemporary architecture of the Amsterdam School (Berlage's followers Kramer and de Klerk for example),[4] while Poelzig's

Chemical Factory at Luban (Posen) of 1912 and the new Stuttgart railway station by Paul Bonatz (1913) may also have influenced Behrens' approach.

The supporting structure of the building is in reinforced concrete, and the roofs are nearly flat, hidden behind a low parapet which is retained at intervals by big wrought iron tie-bars which are made into a bold, medievalizing feature.

At the main entrance, three doors give access to a vestibule in the main block and from here the visitor enters the central hall through a single central opening.

This hall is one of Behrens' most striking inventions. It runs the full height of the building, about 15 metres (50 ft), and is top lit by three enormous star-like sky lights. At either end is a staircase, and the balconies or corridors along the sides at each level are open into the body of the hall. The eight huge pillars that support the balconies transform this conventional arrangement into an extraordinary interior. Each pillar is a stepped triangle in cross-section, each step being one brick deep. The pillars thicken as they rise by an extra cladding of two bricks on every surface. The tiers of vertical steps thus formed, steadily cantilevering outwards as they rise, superficially resemble organ pipes or a paraphrase of the clustered shafts of the crossing piers of a Gothic cathedral. They are, furthermore, coloured.[5]

Behrens described the sequence of colours in a letter to the company's site architect, Fehse, in January 1923. He had been working on the idea during a stay in Vienna (he had by now taken up his post at the Vienna Academy) and he included three sheets of coloured drawings: one a general view, and two showing the juxtaposition of the colours in detail. The design places yellow (the colour of joy, the closest to white light, as Goethe wrote in his Theory of Colours) at the top, next to the crystalline skylights.

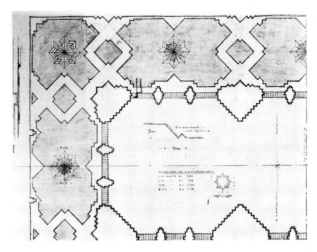

Hoechst: Half-plans of Hall: Ground floor (above line); Upper floor (below).

Hoechst: Interior of Hall.

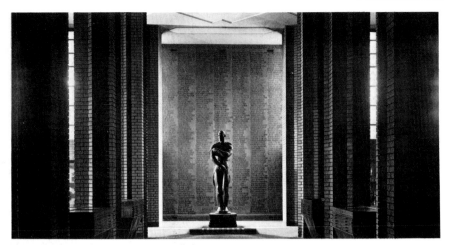

Hoechst: Roll of Honour. Statue by Richard Scheibe.

Following Behrens' written instructions, the central vertical row of bricks at the top was coloured the lightest and brightest yellow; from there the colour deepened and reddened to reach orange in the successive rows on either side. The same orange was then used for the central row of the cluster of steps below, and this orange was deepened in turn step by step to red; the central row below that began with carmine as the brightest and lightest colour, and so on, the colours descending in the order of the spectrum, until the ground floor columns were coloured from green to blue at either side.

There is little doubt that Behrens intended the place to be an exalted and transcendental one; tone and colour climbing from dark, cool blue-green to radiant light. It was planned to work a dramatic effect on the mind of the spectator as he entered the hall. For the view straight ahead was of the bronze memorial figure of a worker by the sculptor Richard Scheibe, standing in the adjacent hall at right angles to the main axis, silhouetted against an enormous white wall painted with the names of some six hundred employees who had been killed in the recent war.

The term occasionally used for the main hall, *Ehrenhalle* (Hall of Honour), makes it clear that the two halls must be seen together as an expiatory and funerary monument, expressive both of tragedy and hope, all the more poignant in the atmosphere generated by the French occupation and the volatile political climate.

Today the colours are largely faded and do not read well. The roll of honour has disappeared so that the immediate message of the bronze figure is subdued. The main hall is powerfully gloomy and oppressive. If it was always so, the architecture may have turned out differently to that intended by the architect and the client.

The lecture theatre on the second floor was damaged during the Second World War, (when the roll of honour also went) and the exhibition area has been rearranged. Some of the sculpture decorating the entrance (by Ludwig Gies) was removed during the Nazi period, as it was apparently expressionist, and therefore considered to be degenerate in character. Two lions in relief, high up, were spared.

The Dombauhütte, Munich

A second building that should be seen in relation to the Hoechst Administration Headquarters was a small brick pavilion for the Munich *Gewerbeschau* (Exhibition of Applied Arts) in 1922.

Behrens' *Dombauhütte* (cathedral's mason's lodge) was a small brick-built rectangular building designed to display church furnishings in a chapel-like atmosphere. The high walls were executed in violent polychromatic brick patterns of interpenetrating chevrons. These continue upwards into the gables, of which there are one at either end and three along each side. The wooden beams of the roof structure protrude through the walls to the exterior of the building and are supported at the corners on pyramidal corbels and on buttresses along the sides. The roof is of vigorous pantiles. Again the whole building is reminiscent of the Amsterdam School.

The interior contained works of religious art by some of the artists about whom Behrens was currently enthusiastic. There was a sarcophagus by Richard Scheibe, a triptych by Adolf Hölzel, a stained glass window by Alfred Partikel. Behrens said in his opening speech:

What we are bringing together can be no more than the carrying out of an exploration. Perhaps, though, we can give through it some stimulation for others, who in better times will carry out greater things.

One of the most striking exhibits was a crucifix by Ludwig Gies, who was also employed by Behrens on the Hoechst building. This crucifix, which Paul Joseph Cremers (in his 1928 book on Behrens) saw as 'the symbol of a whole new direction in art' and which he described with the greatest enthusiasm, raised a storm of controversy at the time of its exhibition, with serious repercussions on Behrens for the future.

The opposition to the crucifix and by association to the *Dombauhütte* came from conservative religious and artistic circles, apparently supported by the National Socialists. The latter were, of course, at their strongest in Munich at that time, with 6,000 members under the freshly achieved leadership of Adolf Hitler. There was, moreover, a marked convergence of religious and Nazi prejudices over a wide range of subjects in Munich. Following violent protests, the crucifix was removed and the *Dombauhütte* itself closed. Behrens himself, as secretary of the exhibition directorate, was obliged to give written consent to the closure. This cause célèbre of the time has been seen as the first dispirited yielding to extremist political interference on the part of the *Werkbund* (which organized the exhibition) and other authorities.[6]

Delayed repercussions from this incident are of interest. The whole affair was dredged up in September and October 1938 by Konrad Nonn (editor of

(Above) Dombauhütte at the Exhibition of Applied Art, Munich, 1922.

(Left) Good Hope Company buildings, Oberhausen, 1921–25.

157

the Prussian Finance Ministry's architectural journal *Zentralblatt der Bauver-waltung*, and scourge, during its existence, of the Bauhaus).[7] At that time the AEG were once more wishing to employ Behrens as architect of a new headquarters to be situated on Hitler and Speer's projected north-south axis for Berlin. Nonn's letters to the *SS-Standartenführer* Rattenhuber, which were passed to Hitler's Adjutant *SS-Gruppenführer* Julius Schaub (for Hitler's personal attention), in a concentrated attempt to frustrate the possibility of Behrens' participation, enclosed photocopies of a page from the *Zeitschrift für Bauwesen* of 1923 showing the interior and exterior of the *Dombauhütte*.

The so-called *Dombauhütte*, in which the blasphemous Christ by Gies, along with other crude works which made a mockery of art and religion, by degenerate artists, was a special undertaking of Professor Peter Behrens.

The crucifix had already, he said, aroused the antagonism of the people in 1921 when it was to be the war memorial of Lübeck Cathedral; the head had been hewn off and thrown into a mill-pond. And yet Peter Behrens had still gathered degenerate artists (Pechstein, Prince Max von Hohenlohe for example) around him. The indignation of the people, wrote Nonn, caused the exhibition to be closed by the police. Behrens had subsequently travelled in Switzerland giving illustrated lectures, he alleged, stirring up an uproar in the Swiss Press 'against German Culture'. The *Dombauhütte* affair was, then, a rare example of Nazi indignation over the character of modern Christian art. Where agitation over art in general is concerned, it anticipated the notorious exhibition of *Entartete Kunst* in Munich in 1937 by fifteen years—an exhibition at which the crucifix of the unfortunate Gies was once more put on view as an example of degenerate art.

Oberhausen: The Gutehoffnungshütte

Although executed during the same period (1921–5) as the two buildings just discussed, the *Gutehoffnungshütte* (Good Hope Company's warehouse) complex at Oberhausen (comprising an administration building, a warehouse, an oil storage tank and a building for the canteen, welfare offices, and so on, of the employees) is quite different in style. The general appearance of the group is Wrightian, with a horizontal emphasis given by flat projecting widely cantilevered roofs, the composition being punctuated by towers with a polychromatic effect of white horizontal concrete bands against the dark brickwork. The structure was a mixture of reinforced concrete and steel, clad in brick, and the warehouse, which was designed to take considerable weights of steel, iron and other materials in storage, was built in five sections on a concrete raft 90 cm (3 ft) thick as a precaution against subsidence as the district is considerably undermined. In the interior, large ceramic tiles were extensively used for both walls and floors. Thorn-Prikker designed a stained glass window for the office building.

Vienna

In 1921, Behrens was called to the Düsseldorf Academy, but after a year he left to become Professor of the Master School for Architecture at the Vienna Academy, following Otto Wagner, who had recently died.[8] Whilst in Vienna (where he was to remain as Professor until 1936) Behrens retained his Berlin home, office and architectural practice. Looking back in 1930, Behrens summarized the aims of his Academic Master School.[9]

Equal in rank and constitution to a university, he explained, the Vienna Academy of Fine Arts, of which his School was a constituent part, offered post-graduate students of architecture from all countries an opportunity to research under the guidance of a Master. Behrens stressed the overall importance of town-planning; of sympathetic co-operation with engineers; of the duty of architects to devise good housing for the masses; of the necessity of an interest in handicraft, and in the integration of painting and sculpture with architecture. He wrote with enthusiasm of the *'neue Sachlichkeit'*:

That quality of essential realism which is native to the thing itself, a vitality independent of extraneous factors; it is at once the physical manifestation of the thing, and an expression of the significance which is attached to it.[10]

The 'free arts', he wrote, 'have been going their own ways in the past decades, and it must be acknowledged that they have resulted in a release of the rhythmical and psychic tensions of our time'.

The statement as a whole is a testament of an 'international modern' standpoint, and suggests that Behrens' attitudes during the late 1920s and early 1930s were in accord with those of his younger colleagues who were to emigrate following the rise of Nazism.

There can be no doubt that the effects of a meeting and mingling of various national qualities and tastes, of the discussion of experiences in construction in different foreign countries, of cultural traditions, all help to inspire the development of modern architecture in a most favourable way.

Hugo Häring, (the Berlin architect and secretary of the association of architects known as the *Ring*) was very impressed by the Viennese Master School, when reviewing an exhibition in Berlin of its activities, held in March 1926:

In Germany there is no Academy, and no Technical College, which can match the spirit of this Viennese School. Young people vibrate with excited longing to shape the future. And in their first fantasies about the future, young people project solely that which elevates their lives. What is clever, and precisely what Behrens does in order to bring this about, is to bring building projects much closer to the young, to inspire contemporary dreams that will bear fruit in the future. We openly admit that Behrens astonishes us. And Germany . . .?[11]

An American architect, William Muschenheim, who was one of Behrens' most brilliant students at this period (he won the Behrens Prize) has recalled:

The principal attribute of his teaching method was that, due to his recognition of the special individual creative abilities of each student, he emphasized that the student must learn how to develop his potentialities and be aware of their relationship to a new era, rather than follow any predetermined rules. He also stressed that students should learn from one another . . . Any work of mine having a kind of significance owes a great debt to my contact with Behrens.[12]

The impression Behrens made on the Austrians was consistent with that he made on so many others during his life. Ernst Plischke, for example, recalled that his friendship was very reserved and restrained. Having worked with English people so long, Plischke thought that Behrens was just like an Englishman. 'Unlike the Viennese', moreover, 'he certainly liked "hard drinks"'. Behrens had evidently long ago drifted away from his ardent teetotalism. Muschenheim also remarked that 'he lived well and at times indulged in spirits'. He was on friendly terms at this period with Josef Hoffmann, the leader of the *Wiener Werkstätte* and with Count Coudenhove-Kalergi, the anti-anti semite and advocate of the 'Pan-Europe' movement.

In the immediate post-war, post-revolutionary years, Vienna had a strong Social Democrat municipal government, which determined to embark on an ambitious programme of officially sponsored housing. To finance this community housing, taxes were levied in 1922 and 1923 especially for the purpose. In September 1923, the municipality set the target of building 25,000 dwellings. (Between this date and 1934, 64,000 units were in fact created). Special attention had to be paid to town planning, hygiene and the general quality of life in the new housing.

A dozen or so architects under the leadership of Karl Ehn, head of the municipality's architectural department were employed on the new schemes, which came to be regarded throughout Europe as the outstanding achievement of the Viennese City Council in setting an example to other cities.

Behrens designed part of the Winarskyhof (Vienna XX) in 1924. This is a large rectangular block of flats which, although cut through by a street, Leystrasse (which is fenced off), is situated as an island in a wide pedestrianized precinct with gardens and children's playgrounds. This in turn is surrounded by a continuous row of apartment blocks by Hoffmann, Frank, Strnad, Wlach and others.[13]

In the same year Behrens designed a housing scheme at Konstanzigasse 44 (Vienna XXII) and a little later (1928) the Franz Domes-Hof, Margaretengürtel 126–134, (Vienna V).

Other work in the early 1920s
Once more, Behrens' range of activities became almost bewilderingly diverse. In addition to the post-war work already discussed, he made

notable designs for the Abbey of St Peter, Salzburg, at the invitation of the Abbot, Petrus Klotz; for the parish church of St Lambert, Essen-Rellinghausen; for the mausoleum of the industrialist Hugo Stinnes at Mullheim; for a new bridge, the Brigitta-Brücke, in Vienna; a villa for Alexander Hoffman in Penzigerstrasse, Vienna; a quayside covered workshop in Barcelona; a head office for the Stumm Concern of Düsseldorf; letter-boxes for the German Post Office; a porcelain service for

Monument for the grave of Friedrich Ebert, 1925.

the State Porcelain Factory in Berlin; the tomb of Friedrich Ebert, the first *Reichspräsident*, on the Waldfriedhof, Heidelberg (the sculptural reliefs by Karl Knappe); the grave of Hans Jäckh at Ida (again using Ludwig Gies as sculptor) and a number of exhibition projects, including the 'Workroom of a Savant' for the Vienna Exhibition of 1923.

Of interest for the history of British architecture was the house Behrens designed for W. J. Basset-Lowke in Northampton. This, 'New Ways', was

New Ways, Northampton, England, 1923–25.

161

the first private house in the 'international modern' style to be built in England. Designed in 1923 and completed by 1925, the house was required by Mr Basset-Lowke to be a single, two-storey block with all the rooms contained within this simple form and under one roof. It also had to incorporate a room from an earlier house, designed by Charles Rennie Mackintosh. The living room had to be large enough for dancing; central heating and electric power in every room were required, although a coal-fire was to be retained as a feature of the living room, in the English manner. The servants were to be accommodated in some comfort: their bedroom was to have hot and cold running water, and they were to have their own sitting room.

The U-shaped plan, with a central door, hall and staircase, and with projecting wings on either side of a loggia on the garden side is familiar Behrens from the time of the Cuno house onwards. The elevations, under a flat roof hidden behind a parapet, are smooth rendered white stucco. The curious detail of small black vertical blocks or rods decorating the parapet all round are perhaps intended to evoke the style of Mackintosh or Hoffmann. The gates and front doors were painted ultramarine blue.

The house was discussed as a great novelty in the *Architectural Review* in October 1926, with the expression of some doubts and many little jokes at the expense of its modernity. Bernard Shaw, who was a guest there once, was asked if he had slept well, and is reported to have replied, 'Yes, thank you. I always sleep with my eyes shut'.

Two Exhibitions

In response to the contemporary enthusiasm for glass as a material—not, hitherto, a special interest of Behrens—two of his exhibition projects of 1925 were largely constructed of glass. One was the rather hectic-looking conser-

vatory for the Austrian pavilion by Hoffmann at the *Grande Exposition des Arts Décoratifs* in Paris, in which too many violent diagonal elements appear to have played a major part, and the pavilion of the *Verein Deutsche Spiegel-glasfabriken* (Union of German Mirror-glass manufacturers) for a Cologne exhibition. The latter is a delightful essay in the visionary-crystalline manner of Scheerbart or Taut.

Behrens was indeed increasingly tending to follow modes in architecture pioneered by his contemporaries and juniors. His 1926 design for a hotel, the Ritz in Brünn (today Brno), is distinctly reminiscent of Mies van der Rohe's Office Building project for Friedrichstrasse in Berlin (1921) or Fritz Höger's *Chilehaus*, Hamburg (1922–3). The perspective drawings emanating from Behrens' office (admittedly not all from his own hand) are all, in the late 1920s, in the smudgy, slightly expressionist style then fashionable among German architects. A little later, the racy, violently fluid black-and-white style of Erich Mendelsohn was even adopted.

In 1923–4, the *Zehner-Ring*, or Circle of Ten was formed in Germany, and a little later this was expanded to form an association of twenty-six or seven architects (among them Taut, May, Gropius, Mies, Mendelsohn and others) who joined forces in order to publish statements in the professional journals, to hold group exhibitions and so on. Behrens became a member of the *Ring* as it was subsequently known, having also been, since its formation in 1924, a member of the council of management of the Circle of Friends of the Bauhaus along with such non-architect figures as Chagall, Kokoschka, Werfel and Einstein. Together with his participation in the *Novembergruppe* mentioned earlier, these memberships and associations make it clear that Behrens was in accord throughout the 1920s with the liberal, modernist and progressive elements in his profession.

(Opposite) Exposition des Arts Décoratifs, Paris, 1925: Viennese Pavilion Conservatory.

(Left) German Mirror-Glass Manufacturers' Pavilion, Cologne, 1925. Drawing.

163

The Weissenhofsiedlung, Stuttgart

The *Werkbund* exhibition *Die Wohnung* of 1927 in Stuttgart consisted, as is well known, of a group of houses and apartment blocks by invited artists under the general direction of Ludwig Mies van der Rohe. Although Mies avoided the imposition of a strict control over the types of housing to be shown, he made it clear that he wanted the architects to 'make their contribution to the problem of the modern dwelling', and there is no doubt that he had the problems of economy, rationalization and standardization in mind. The houses were to be prototypes of potentially mass-produced dwellings. (It is obvious that some of the participants, Bourgeois and Scharoun, for example, did not take this too seriously.) The houses had also to be properly constructed, permanent dwellings, for sale after the exhibition period.

Behrens contributed a development of his *Terrassenhaus* idea; as he put it:

The Terrace-House I projected is arranged as a conglomerate of single, two, three and four-storey apartments, which are fitted together in such a way that the flat roof of the lower apartment offers the terrace for the one lying above and behind it.[14]

The Behrens *Terrassenhaus* was built on Hölzelweg 3–5, and comprised twelve units of accommodation: eight three-roomed apartments (for 3–4 persons) and four with four rooms (for five or six persons). The walls were built of hollow blocks, stuccoed, and the floors were reinforced concrete. The apartments had hot water central heating and compared well for economy with those, for example, of Le Corbusier in the same scheme. A comparison of the four-roomed apartments of an area of 60 sq metres (645 sq ft) by both architects shows those of Behrens to have cost 1·30 Reichsmark per square metre, whilst those of Le Corbusier cost 4·30 Reichsmark.[15]

The *Weissenhofsiedlung* suffered damage during the Second World War, and the Behrens *Terrassenhaus* was heavily remodelled with pitched roofs.

The last years

Other, unexecuted projects of 1927 were for a harbour-slipway in Tilsit; an entry in the competition for an extension to the Reichstag building; an entry, which won first prize, for a new bridge over the Rhine between Cologne and Müllheim.[16] The year 1928 saw the design of a domed synagogue at Zilina, Czechoslovakia, and the beginning of Behrens' designs for the rearrangement of Alexanderplatz in Berlin.

A major retrospective exhibition of his work was held in Berlin to commemorate his sixtieth birthday, and Paul-Joseph Cremers published his monograph reviewing the work of Behrens up to the time of writing. In 1929, Behrens submitted designs and a model for the *Centrosoyus* (Co-operative Society) headquarters in Moscow. This project, for a huge building to house 2,800 office workers had been the subject of a limited competition, to which Max Taut and Le Corbusier were also invited. Behrens' compact and powerful block, somewhat on the same lines as a 1923 design

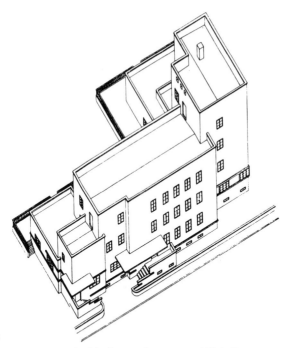

Terrace block at the Weissenhofsiedlung, Stuttgart, 1926–7.

for a Stock Exchange in Cologne, is less well known than the winning design by Le Corbusier.

At this period, Behrens was often in direct competition with much younger architects, including his former assistants. He won the competition for the design of Alexanderplatz, for which five other architects (including the Luckhardt brothers and Mies van der Rohe) were invited to submit plans within guidelines laid down by the Berlin City architect, Martin Wagner. Behrens' scheme was to surround the square with a unified but irregular composition of large discontinuous office blocks, some curved, some angled in plan, with a linking theme of wholly glass penthouses and towers dramatically inserted into the solid blocks of the buildings, with closely spaced vertical fin-like mullions between the windows. This idea perhaps developed from his observation of the closed, formal effect of the tall narrow mullions of the Mannesmann building (or the Hoechst building) when seen from an oblique angle—an effect Behrens particularly remarked upon.

The project was really crushed by the economic crisis of the early 1930s, and discontinued after the rise of Hitler, partly because of the hostility of the new régime to Martin Wagner. In the event, the only part of the scheme to be built (1930–31) were two modest, emasculated blocks on the south-west side of the new square, with the beginning of Rathausstrasse between them. Today they survive in a badly mangled area of East Berlin; they are dull and characterless buildings in the close company of the grotesquely inflated

165

House for Professor Dr Kurt Lewin, Berlin, 1929–30.

(Left) Place setting of cutlery designed by Behrens, 1930.

(Below) Villa Clara Ganz, Cronberg in the Taunus mountains, 1931.

(Bottom) Villa Clara Ganz. Plans: (bottom left) ground floor; (bottom right) upper floor.

167

derivations of this style of office block that were built along the nightmarish Karl-Marx Allee nearby, after the Second World War.

In 1930, Behrens made a number of careful and sensitive designs for a war memorial (unexecuted) to be created inside Schinkel's *Neue Wache* on Unter den Linden. He was able to realize some pleasant luxury apartment blocks on the corner of Bolivarallee and Eichenallee (Westend, Berlin) which have survived, and the substantial and handsome *Haus* Lewin in Schlachtensee, near the lake.[17] In keeping with the design of this cubic architecture is one of the finest of Behrens' late works of applied art—a dinner service of cutlery (1930) executed by the *Deutsche Werkstätte*.

In June 1930, he was instrumental in forming the *Reichsverband für deutsche Wertarbeit* (National Union for German Quality Work) which attempted to carry on a Werkbund programme independently of political interference, and which survived until about 1934.

A Villa in the Taunus Mountains

Among the really large, luxurious villas that were built in the early 1930s (the best known of which are those of Mies van der Rohe and Le Corbusier), the villa for Clara Ganz near Cronberg by Behrens has a respectable place. Although it is not perhaps as imaginative or innovatory as the villas by his former assistants, it is a well-proportioned, strongly composed articulation of cubic forms; a house built on a hillside with generous terraces on all sides, and with a terraced garden carefully related to the whole composition. Linking the two-storey sections at either end of the house (one end is a garage with a chauffeur's apartment above) is a very broad terrace over the kitchens and servants' quarters.

The house was constructed of brick and faced with thin slabs of white limestone from the quarries of Freyburg an-der-Unstrut, a stone with attractive weathering properties. The flat surfaces are flagged with artificial stone to match the walls, and the garden, designed by Camillo Schneider in collaboration with the architect, falls away in terraces retained by roughly dressed drystone walls of slaty limestone.

The interior was very lavishly decorated when first completed; the living room walls were lined with parchment, while the floor was dark ebonized bog-oak into which was laid a pattern of lines in white maple. The dining-room walls and ceiling were panelled in rosewood, and the window was made to slide away (in the manner of the one at the Tugendhat house by Mies) so that the space was continuous with the terrace. A blown-air central heating system was used. The house was empty and fell into disrepair after the Second World War, and was vandalized. It has since been restored, but very much altered.

The Ring der Frauen

Still able to surprise, Behrens designed a delightful little pavilion for the German Building Exhibition of 1931, which was held on the exhibition

Ring der Frauen pavilion, Building Exhibition, Berlin, 1931.

grounds near Karolingerplatz in Berlin. (Behrens was also responsible for the general layout of the exhibition). The *Ring der Frauen* (Women's Circle) was a circular hall some 18 metres (58 ft) in diameter and 5 metres (16 ft) high, around which three circular satellite rooms were grouped, one of which was the entrance hall. The floors of the two smaller circular rooms were higher than that of the main hall, and as they were wide open to it, they might serve, Behrens wrote, for theatrical performances or for music. On the side of the building opposite the entrance was a wide opening on to a terrace for open-air displays or for dancing. The *Ring der Frauen* was a prototype for a women's cultural centre or institute. The white, tiled exterior, with its wide, curved horizontal windows, its flat roofs and circular fountain on the segment of terrace make this one of the most attractive little buildings of the period. It was possibly a source of inspiration for Charles Holden's Arnos Grove Underground Station in London the following year.

Behrens' last great industrial building (1932–34) was the cigarette factory at Linz for the Austrian State Tobacco Company, which was designed in collaboration with Alexander Popp. A six-storey steel-framed structure with a long, continuous convex façade, following the Ludlgasse, it has unbroken ribbons of steel-framed windows running the entire length. The general effect is reminiscent of the work of Mendelsohn.

During the Third Reich
In 1932, the Austrian *Werkbund*, which was closely linked to the German

parent association, mounted an exhibition of model housing along the lines of the *Weissenhofsiedlung* at Stuttgart. The aims of the exhibition were in fact slightly different, but there were obvious similarities of style, and there was the same internationalism. Architects such as Häring, Lurçat and Rietveld were invited by Josef Frank, who was responsible for the general direction. The exhibition led directly to a split in the Austrian *Werkbund*, from which the then President, Hermann Neubacher (a National Socialist and future *Burgermeister* of Vienna), resigned in protest against, among other things, the 'Semiticization' of the *Werkbund*—an attack on Frank.

After an Extraordinary General Meeting in July 1933 and much further trouble, a new *Werkbund* was established in Austria the following year, with Clemens Holzmeister as President and with Peter Behrens and Josef Hoffmann as Vice-Presidents. Jews and socialists were excluded from the membership of the new *Werkbund*, in line with the German parent organization, which was by now under National Socialist leadership and to all intents and purposes extinct.[18] The general political climate in Austria moved sharply to the right at this time, as Dolfuss suspended parliamentary government and proceeded to crush the Socialists. The *Werkbund* President Holzmeister became his official advisor on art and design.

It is not clear what Behrens' motives were in associating himself with such an organization as the Austrian *Werkbund* in its reconstituted form. William Muschenheim, then his pupil, remembers him as 'clearly not in agreement with what was occurring in Germany and Austria in regard to a rising Nazism'. It is perhaps charitable to assume that, like many German conservatives who made every effort to remain in positions of power within their professional organizations in the face of National Socialist take-over, he hoped to act as a moderating influence on events until such time as things returned to normal.

There is little doubt, however, that Behrens made some attempts, however belated and tentative, to ingratiate himself with the new powers in Germany. In a statement connected with his *Vorschlag zur Ernennung* (Application for Appointment) of 1939 given to the *Akademie der Künste* in Berlin (a formal application for the renewal of his contract), he claimed to have actually joined the then illegal Austrian NSDAP on 1 May 1934. In the form which Behrens completed in 1939 there is, however, no entry in the column for Party Membership Number, which virtually invalidates the claim. Albert Speer, who was surprised to hear that Behrens was ever a Nazi, is of the opinion that Behrens, knowing that the records of the Austrian party, during its illegal phase, were sketchy or non-existent, was using this rather insubstantial claim to political affiliation as a safeguard. Perhaps, like many a *Mitläufer* he simply paid a subscription in 1934 as an insurance policy.

In 1933, he published an appreciative article entitled *'Die Baugesinnung des Faschismus'* ('The Fascist approach to architecture') in the fashionable magazine *Die Neue Linie*.[19] This article was essentially a report on the fifth Milan Triennale, and a review of ten years of architectural activity under the

Fascist régime in Italy. While the article was quite wrongly pitched to stir the heart of a bona fide fanatical National Socialist (it is illustrated exclusively with photographs of fairly mundane, bourgeois objects such as golf club-houses, hotels and attractive villas, all with white walls and flat roofs), Nationalism is revealed in the pride expressed in the derivation from the Germans of the style (the Italians call it *'tipo tedesco'*, he wrote), in preference to the 'trivially playful, decorative French approach'; and he used a cult word of the Nazis, *völkisch* (truly of the people), however inappropriately, for the awakening spirit of the Italian people evinced by the exhibition.

Behrens was unsuccessful with his entry for a competition to design a Congress, Sport and Exhibition Hall on the Heiligengeistfelde in Hamburg in 1934. His submission was prepared with Alexander Popp and the engineer Robert Schindler. Fritz Höger also took part in this competition.[20]

Opposition to his continued activity as an architect began to grow, and from sources dangerously close to home. A letter (of 22 February 1934) from a former assistant in his Berlin office, Werner Fechner, illustrates the atmos-phere of menace surrounding Behrens at this time. The letter was to Win-fried Wendland (by now Deputy Leader of the *Werkbund*) at the Ministry of Culture. It poured scorn on 'Professor Behrens' apparent desire to be recon-ciled to the National Socialist régime', which Fechner regarded as 'most surprising'. He enclosed with his letter, by way of proof of Behrens' true attitude to National Socialism, a couple of other documents.

One was a copy of a denunciation that he, Fechner, had written to the NSDAP headquarters of the *Gau Gross-Berlin* in July 1932. This denunciation is a somewhat garbled account of his allegedly unfair dismissal from Behrens' office; he claimed that he was given the sack, two hours after having been overheard making his political sympathies clear to a colleague. He quoted examples of other colleagues and assistants being given notice for the same reason. The direct agent of these dismissals had been, he alleged, a 'Viennese gentleman' appointed by Behrens to be in charge of the Berlin office. Conflict with an equally un-named 'gracious lady of the house (she is a Jewess)' is also rather obscurely cited. Although this letter does little more than to convey an expression of ill-focused vindictiveness, it was accom-panied on its way to Wendland's desk with a strongly supporting testimony by Karl Mittel, a longstanding and important assistant to Behrens. Fechner's case was typical of many he had seen occur in Behrens' house, he affirmed; Fechner had been a useful and conscientious colleague. 'Things had hap-pened', he wrote, 'that are not uninteresting in present-day circumstances!' Although, he concluded, he recognized Behrens as an artist, problem-solver and architect of the avant-garde of our times, he despised him as a man and as a character.[21]

The last work
In 1936, Behrens returned to Berlin to take an academic post as head of the Master School of Architecture at the *Akademie der Künste*, following the death

Headquarters for the AEG, North-South Axis, Berlin, 1937–9: Model. Behrens' building is on the extreme left of photo.

of Hans Poelzig. Little of substance remains of this appointment other than a file of mistrustful official enquiries into his military service of so long ago, his previous political affiliations, his former membership of the Rotary Club and so on. He was not given permission to visit Vienna during the winter semester of 1937–38: 'the class', he was simply told, 'cannot be permitted'.[22] Nevertheless, he still was striving in some degree to conform. According to Joan Campbell, the art historian Edwin Redslob 'although a long-time friend and neighbour of Behrens, came to shun him in the 1930s for his pro-Nazi sympathies'. His letters of the period are signed with the grotesque salutation encouraged by the Nazis, *'Mit deutschem Gruss. Heil Hitler!'* So were those of his wife, Lilli.[23]

The question of a new headquarters for the AEG arose during the latter part of the decade, when Albert Speer was entrusted with the general planning of a new *Nord-Süd Achse* (north-south axis) for Berlin, to run from an enormous domed hall near the old Reichstag building in the north, to a new central railway station near the Tempelhof air field in the south. It was decided that the headquarters of the principal Berlin industrial concerns should be on this new avenue, which would complement and cross the east-west axis of Unter den Linden and the Strasse des 17 Juni. According to Speer, the then general manager of the AEG, Dr Bücher, expressed the desire to have Peter Behrens as the architect for their building.

Again, a violent attack was made on Behrens. Konrad Nonn made desperate attempts to prevent the possibility.

Behrens is widely known in architectural circles as a Bolshevist. If Peter Behrens can actually attach himself close to the Führer, we will be a laughing-stock among the cultural bolshevists. . . . I believe it to be of burning importance for the Führer to be informed of what is stacked up against him . . .

Nonn's letter brought up Behrens' previous association with 'Communists and Jews: Albert Einstein, Franz Werfel, etc.' and the fact that he had helped to organize the fiftieth birthday party of Herwarth Walden, the Jewish director of the *Sturm* gallery in Berlin. His friendship with the Rathenaus and with Martin Wagner, the former Berlin architect, was also brought up in the dossier. Copies of all this were put before Wilhelm Frick, the Minister of the Interior and the lawyers Neumann and Beneke, as well as Hitler himself.[24]

According to Speer, who retained a certain repect for some of the architects of the previous generation, he was able to protect Behrens against these attacks by being, as was his shrewd custom, the first to gain Hitler's ear on matters in which he was interested, and so to obtain an irreversible decision on them.[25] In any case, Nonn's attack was probably an indirect attack on Speer as well. In his letter of October 1938 to Rattenhuber, he mentions a list of 'Bolshevist' architects he had circulated earlier.

Most of them, as Jews and convinced Bolshevists, have, moreover, emigrated. But Professor Peter Behrens appears to have succeeded in getting himself close to the Führer—I can guess how, but can't say right out.

'I was able', remarked Speer recently, 'to get Nonn the sack'.[26] Hitler, he has reported, knew of the St Petersburg Embassy and liked it. This was enough to silence the opposition.[27]

The design of the AEG building was made in conjunction with the architect Eugen Himmel and completed by October 1939, but was never executed. It was on one of the best sites and would have been one of the first buildings to be constructed. One of the curious conditions of the whole *Nord-Süd Achse* scheme was that, in order to save steel for rearmament, all construction had to be without steel or reinforced concrete; it was to be of masonry and wood in the eighteenth-century manner. It would have been a huge building, housing 4,000 office workers, and the principal façade would have been some 225 metres (737 ft) long. It was a rather lifeless variant of the *Continental-Caoutchouc* building, in style. Speer remembers Behrens as a sick man, with an inhaler. He came to discussions accompanied by his daughter Petra. He was unhappy, Speer feels, with the design, and the whole set-up.[28]

Behrens had suffered heart trouble for many years, from as early as 1905. He died of a heart attack on the 27 February 1940, aged seventy-two years. His death was hardly remarked upon in the newspapers of the time. His death mask was taken by his friend the sculptor, Richard Scheibe. He was cremated at Wilmersdorf on 5 March, and Amersdorffer, President of the Berlin *Academie der Künste* read an address.

Notes

1. Peter Behrens, *'Wiederaufbau der deutschen Baukunst'*, *Westdeutsche Wochenschrift für Politik*, I, 1919.

2. His work was appreciatively noted in Paul Fechter's review in the *Deutsche Allgemeine Zeitung* 21 May 1926.

3. In a letter of 3 August 1921: *Dokumente aus Hoechster Archiven, 4: Peter Behrens schuf Turm und Brücke*, Hoechst, Farbwerke Hoechst, 1964.

4. See Stanford Anderson op. cit., p432, n13. Behrens must also have known of the contemporary brick revival in Hamburg, and of Fritz Schumacher's *Das Wesen des neuzeitlichen Backsteinbau* (The modern technique of brick construction), 1920.

5. Behrens was a signatory to a call for colour in architecture: *'Aufruf zum farbigen Bauen!' Die Bauwelt*, Yr. 10, No. 38, 18 September 1919.

6. See Joan Campbell *Werkbund* op. cit., p155ff.

7. The letters of Nonn, as well as those from Fechner, Mittel et al quoted further on, are in the Behrens file in the Berlin Document Center, Berlin.

8. Wagner won one of the first prizes for his entry in the competition to design the Emperor Franz Josef Municipal Museum on the Schmeltz in 1912, 'thanks to the persistent advocacy of Peter Behrens, one of the adjudicators'.

9. Karl Maria Grimme, *Peter Behrens und seine Wiener Akademische Meisterschule*, Vienna, Luser, 1930. This has a parallel English text.

10. The previous year, however, he had expressed doubts about the *neue Sachlichkeit*. In a letter to August Hoff at the Duisburger Museums Verein, 26 February 1929, he expressed his enthusiasm for working for the Church, which he felt stood as a bulwark against the materialism and all too great *neue Sachlichkeit* of modern times, which he feared led easily to a sort of spiritless and soulless mechanical circus. He also, in this letter, expressed his longing to build something in his home town, Hamburg. The letter is partially published in *Peter Behrens (1868–1940), Gedenkschrift mit Katalog*, Pfalzgalerie Kaiserslautern, 1966, p10.

11. *Peter Behrens Gedenkschrift mit Katalog* op. cit., p30.

12. Letter to the author from William Muschenheim, Ann Arbor, of 26 March 1980. Plischke's remarks are from *'Gedanken zu Peter Behrens'*, *Bauforum 5–6*, Vienna, 1968, pp15–17. Ernst A. Plischke, b 1903, was a pupil of Behrens, an assistant of Josef Frank, and architect of many works in New Zealand. He succeeded to the Chair of Architecture in Vienna in 1963.

13. Within a rectangular area bounded by Stromstrasse, Pasettistrasse, Kaiserwasserstrasse and Vorgartenstrasse. See Ottokar Uhl, *Moderne Architektur in Wien, von Otto Wagner bis Heute*, Vienna, Schrollverlag, 1966, pp48–9, 74–5.

14. Peter Behrens, *'Terrassen am Hause: Deutscher Werkbund'*, *Bau und Wohnung*, Stuttgart, 1927.

15. Jürgen Joedicke and Christian Plath, *Die Weissenhofsiedlung*, Stuttgart, Krämer, 1977.

16. Behrens entry was called *'Aus einem Guss'* ('From the same mould') and was published in *Der Bauingenieur*, Yr. 8, No. 15, Berlin, 1927, pp263–9.

17. See *Berlin und seine Bauten, Teil IV, Band C., Wohnungsbau*, op. cit., p241.

18. See Lucius Burckhardt (Ed.), *Werkbund, Germania, Austria, Svizzera*, Venice, Alfieri, 1977, pp110–11.

19. Peter Behrens, '*Die Baugesinnung des Faschismus*', *Die Neue Linie*, November 1933, pp11–13; another similar article was '*Neue Italienischen Bauten*' in the same magazine, January 1938, pp36–8.

20. See *Deutsche Bauzeitung*, September 1938, p259.

21. Behrens file in the Berlin Document Center, Berlin.

22. Behrens file in the *Akademie der Künste*, Berlin.

23. Behrens file in the *Akademie der Künste*, which contains a number of letters from Behrens and his wife of this period.

24. Behrens file in the Berlin Document Centre. Behrens had known Walden since 1909. He protested against Walden's dismissal from the editorship of *Der Neue Weg* in March 1909.

25. Albert Speer, *Inside the Third Reich*, London, Weidenfeld and Nicholson, 1970, p212. Behrens also designed a new Embassy for Washington in 1936.

26. Albert Speer, in a conversation with the author, 18 April 1980.

27. See also Giovanni K. Koenig, '*Behrens e Dintori*', *Casabella*, 347, Yr. XXXIV, April 1970, p2. This article is a little naïve, perhaps.

28. Speer's assistant, Rudolf Wolters, remembers Behrens as an ever-enthusiastic architect, who wanted to go on working. He was, however, old, reserved, and 'a broken man'. Letter to the author, 10 December 1979.

Bibliography

1. Books, Exhibition Catalogues, Special numbers of Periodicals, Biographical entries, etc, on Behrens

Anderson, S. O., *Peter Behrens and the New Architecture of Germany, 1900–1917*, Columbia University Ph.D. Thesis, 1968. (Available through University Microfilms International).

Branchesi, L., *Peter Behrens*, Rome, Ph.D. Thesis, 1965.

Buddensieg, T., *Peter Behrens und die AEG: Neue Dokumente zur Baugeschichte der Fabriken am Humbolthain*, Munich, Deutscher Kunstverlag, 1975; (Festschrift für Margarete Kühn.)

Buddensieg, T., and Rogge, H., *Industriekultur: Peter Behrens und die AEG, 1907–1914*, Exhibition Catalogue, Milan, Electa, 1978.

Buddensieg, T., and Rogge, H., *Industriekultur: Peter Behrens und die AEG 1907–1914*. Berlin, Mann, 1979.

Casabella June 1960, No. 240. 'Numero dedicato a Peter Behrens'. (Contributions from E. N. Rogers, V. Gregotti etc.)

Cremers, P. J., *Peter Behrens. Sein Werk von 1909 bis zur Gegenwart*, Essen, Baedecker, 1928.

Dokumente aus Hoechster Archiv. Heft 4. Hoechst, Hoechst AG, 1964.

Ehmcke, F. H., *Peter Behrens*, Neue Deutsche Biographie II 1955.

Gerber, W., *Nicht Gebaute Architektur. Peter Behrens und Fritz Schumacher als Kirchenplaner in Hagen. Beispiele aus den Jahren 1906–1907*, Hagen, Linnepe, 1980.

Hesse-Frielinghaus, H., *Peter Behrens und Karl Ernst Osthaus. Eine Dokumentation nach den Beständen des Osthaus-Archivs im Karl-Ernst-Osthaus-Museum, Hagen*, Hagen, 1966.

Hoeber, F., *Peter Behrens*, Munich, Müller & Rentsch, 1913.

Hoepfner, W., and Neumeyer, F., *Das Haus Wiegand von Peter Behrens in Berlin-Dahlem*, Mainz, Phillipp von Zabern, 1979.

Jessen, Hans B., *Der Baumeister Peter Behrens, 1868–1940*, Nordelbingen, vol. 37, Heide in Holstein, Boyens, 1968.

Kadatz, H.-J., *Peter Behrens, Architekt, Maler, Grafiker und Formgestalter, 1868–1940*, Leipzig, 1977.

Lanzke, H., *Peter Behrens, 50 Jahre Gestaltung in der Industrie*, Berlin, AEG, 1958.

Norberg-Schulz, C., *Casa Behrens, Darmstadt*, Rome, Officina Edizione, 1980.

Posener, J., and Imbert, J., *Peter Behrens*. A special number of *Architecture d'Aujourd'hui* Yr. 5, Série 4, no. 2, March 1934.

Shand, P. Morton, 'Scenario for a Human Drama, Part III, Peter Behrens', *Architectural Review*, September 1934; reprinted in a special number of the *AAJ*, 'P. Morton Shand'; *Architectural Association Journal*, No. 827, January 1959.

2. General, Architecture and Design

Architektenzeichnungen, 1479–1979, Exhibition catalogue, Berlin, Kunstbibliothek, 1979.

Banham, R., *Theory and Design in the First Machine Age*, London, The Architectural Press, 1960.

Berlin und Seine Bauten, Berlin, Ernst, 1877–1896–1970–1971–1974 (revised editions).

Borsi, F. and Koenig, G. K., *Architettura dell'Espressionismo*, Genoa, Vitali e Ghianda, 1967.

Bergius, B., Frecot, J., and Radicke, D. (Eds.), *Architektur, Stadt und Politik: Julius Posener zum 75 Geburtstag*, Giessen, Anabas, 1979.

Bott, G. (Ed.), *Von Morris zum Bauhaus: Eine Kunst gegründet auf Einfachkeit*, Hanau, Peters, 1977.

Burckhardt, L. (Ed.), *Werkbund: Germania, Austria, Svizzera*. Venice, La Biennale di Venezia, 1977.

Campbell, J., *The German Werkbund. The politics of reform in the Applied Arts*, Princeton, 1978.

Catalogue of Drawings Collection of the RIBA, Farnborough, Gregg, 1972.

Ein Dokument Deutscher Kunst. Darmstadt 1901–1976, Exhibition Catalogue, 5 vols, Darmstadt, Roether, 1977.

Franciscono, M., *Walter Gropius and the Creation of the Bauhaus in Weimar*, Illinois, UIP, 1971.

Fratini, F. R. (Ed.), *Torino 1902*, Turin, Martano, 1970.

Funk, Anna-Christa, *Karl Ernst Osthaus gegen Hermann Muthesius*, Hagen, KEO Museum, 1978.

Gysling-Billeter, E., *Objekte des Jugendstils*, Bern, Benteli, 1975.

Hermann, W., *Deutsche Baukunst des 19 & 20-er Jahrhunderts* (reprint), Basel, Birkhäuser, 1977.

Hesse-Frielinghaus, H., *Briefwechsel Le Corbusier-Karl Ernst Osthaus*, Hagen, KEO Museum, 1977.

Hitchcock, H.-R., *Architecture, 19th & 20th Centuries*, London, Pelican, 1963.

Joedicke, J., and Plath, C., *Die Weissenhofsiedlung Stuttgart*, Stuttgart, Krämer, 1977.

Kliemann, H., *Die Novembergruppe*, Berlin, 1969.

Kornwolf, J. D., *M. H. Baillie-Scott and the Arts and Crafts Movement*, Baltimore, John Hopkins, 1972.

Lane, B. Miller, *Architecture and Politics in Germany, 1918–1945*, Harvard, 1968.

Madsden, T., *Art Nouveau*, New York, Da Capo, 1975.

Massobrio, G., and Portoghesi, P., *Album degli anni Venti*, Rome, Laterza, 1970.

Messina, M. G., *Darmstadt 1901/1908: Olbrich e la colonia degli artisti*, Rome, Kappa, 1978.

Mosel, C., *Kunsthandwerk im Umbruch*, Hanover, 1971.

Müller-Wulckow, W., *Architektur der Zwanziger Jahre in Deutschland*, (reprint of the four *Blaue Bücher*), Konigstein, Langewiesche & Köster, 1975.

Petsch, J., *Baukunst und Stadtplanung im Dritten Reich*, Munich, Hanser Verlag, 1976.

Raack, H., *Das Reichstagsgebäude in Berlin*, Berlin, Mann, 1978.

Rave, R., and Knöfel, H.-J., *Bauen seit 1900 in Berlin*, Berlin, Kiepert, 1968.

Simon, H.-U., *Sezessionismus. Kunstgewerbe in literarischer und bildender Kunst*, Stuttgart, Metzler, 1976.

Schmutzler, R., *Art Nouveau*, Stuttgart, Hatje, 1977.

Selz, P. and Constantine, M. (Eds.), *Art Nouveau*, New York, MoMA, 1960.

Teut, A., *Architektur im Dritten Reich. 1933–45*, Gütersloh, Bertelsmann, 1967.

Tummers, Nic, *Der Hagener Impuls: J. L. M. Lauweriks, Werk und Einfluss auf Architektur und Formgebung um 1910*, Hagen, Linnepe, 1972.

Tendenzen der 20er Jahre, Exhibition Catalogue, Berlin, Reimer, 1977.

Weber, H., *Walter Gropius und das Faguswerk*, Munich, Callwey, 1961.

Wingler, H. M., *The Bauhaus*, Cambridge, Mass, MIT, 1968.

Whittick, A., *European Architecture in the Twentieth Century*, 2 vols, London, Crosby Lockwood, 1950–3.

Zwischen Kunst und Industrie: Der Deutsche Werkbund, Exhibition Catalogue, Munich, Die Neue Sammlung, 1975.

3. Political, Social and Literary history, Memoirs

Balfour, M., *The Kaiser and his Times*, London, Penguin, 1975.

Carsten, F. L., *The Rise of Fascism*, London, Methuen, 1967.

Dehmel, R., *Ausgewählte Briefe 1883–1902*, Berlin, S. Fischer, 1922.

Dehmel, R., *Ausgewählte Briefe 1902–1920*, Berlin, S. Fischer, 1923.

Diederichs, E., *Selbstzeugnisse und Briefe aus Zeitgenossen*, Düsseldorf, Diederichs, 1967.

Gay, Peter, *Weimar Culture*, London, Penguin, 1968.

Gay, Peter, *Freud, Jews and Other Germans*, New York, OUP, 1978.

Gropius, W., *Apollo in der Demokratie*, Mainz, Florian Kupferberg, 1967.

Grunberger, R., *A Social History of the Third Reich*, London, Weidenfeld and Nicholson, 1971.

Hartleben, O. E., *Briefe von O. E. Hartleben an Freunde*, Berlin, Fischer, 1912.

Hartleben, O. E., *Briefe an seine Frau 1887–1905*, Berlin, Fischer, 1908.

Hesse-Frielinghaus, H. et al, *Karl Ernst Osthaus, Leben und Werk*, Reckling-hausen, Bongers, 1978.

Joll, J., *Three Intellectuals in Politics*, New York, Pantheon, 1961.

Kessler, Harry Graf, *Walther Rathenau*, Berlin, Klemm, 1928; New York, Harcourt, Brace, 1930.

Kessler, H. G., *Tagebücher 1918–1937*. Frankfurt, Insel, 1961. Trans: *Diaries of a Cosmopolitan 1918–1937*, London, Weidenfeld & Nicholson, 1971.

Rathenau, Walther, *Briefe. Neue Folge*, Dresden, Reissner, 1928.

Scheffler, K., *Die fetten und die mageren Jahre*, Leipzig, 1946.

Stern, F., *The Politics of Cultural Despair*, Berkeley, University of California, 1961.

Speer, A., *Inside the Third Reich*, London, Weidenfeld and Nicholson, 1971.

Wem gehört die Welt. Kunst und Gesellschaft in der Weimarer Republik, Exhibition Catalogue, Berlin, NGBK, 1977.

Picture acknowledgements

AEG: 47, 49, 81, 82, 84 (top), 86 (bottom), 88, 96, 97; Architectural Press: 161 (bottom), 167 (middle and bottom); Author's collection: 43 (bottom), 110, 118, 128, 133, 166; Cremers: 162; Hoeber: 10, 19, 21, 22, 29, 32, 51 (top), 59, 61, 63, 66, 67, 71, 72, 73, 101, 102, 108, 114, 116, 121, 122, 130, 131, 134, 136, 138; Hoechst: 150, 151, 153, 154, 155; Kadatz: 163; Klingspor: 28, 40, 42, 43 (top), 44; Kappa: 35, 38; Krämer: 165; Licht: 107; Mann: 86 (top), 100, 132 (top), 144 (middle); Pfalzgalerie Kaiserslautern: 5, 7 (top left), 9, 12, 51 (bottom), 84 (bottom), 70, 132 (bottom), 144 (bottom), 157, 161 (top), 167 (top), 169, 174; Putnams: 8; A. Speer: 172; Stoedtner: 80; Werkbund Archiv: 57.

Index

References in italic are to pages with illustrations

185